THE MESSAGE of the NEW TESTAMENT

EPHESIANS—COLOSSIANS

by THOMAS H. OLBRICHT

Published by
BIBLICAL RESEARCH PRESS
1334 Ruswood
Abilene, Texas
79601

THE MESSAGE OF THE NEW TESTAMENT

EPHESIANS—COLOSSIANS
T.H. OLBRICHT

Library of Congress Catalog Card No. 82-74323
ISBN 0-89112-170-6

Contents

Acknowledgements

This book is possible for various reasons; first, because the Father of our Lord Jesus Christ provided the basis for the contents. Second, it is possible because Abilene Christian University and my immediate supervisor Edward M. Brown enabled me to be released from responsibilities so I could write free from distraction. Third, I am indebted to the elders, deacons and members of the body of the Lord in Glenwood Springs, Colorado. Jack and Linda Hicks arranged for us to spend six weeks with the church and teach Ephesians on Sunday Morning. The supportiveness of those in the class has done much to make this book a labor of love. But we are especially indebted to Pat, Patsy, Jess, and Jodie Dowdy who arranged a delightful and isolated site for our travel trailer so writing could proceed with dispatch. Then last and not least, I am indebted to Dorothy and Erika who shared these weeks and missed many a delightful mountain stream, and the sun breaking in on a snow tipped peak so a manuscript could be forth-coming. I must not forget J. D. Thomas, colleague and mentor, who invited me to write this book. To him I an indebted for this opportunity to get to know Paul better, and to grow personally in a profounder understanding of the gospel.

Cattle Creek Canyon, Colorado
June 29, 1982

Chapter 1

PAUL, THE MESSAGE, THE SETTING

In March, 62 A.D. a unique group made its way along the rock paved Appian Way leading into Rome. It was not an unusual group in appearance. The city of Rome, its population approaching a million, was accustomed to frequent military and foreign contingents entering and exiting from the city. This group would have attracted little attention. What made this particular company unique was the presence of a wizened, but still vigorous Jew above 60 by the name of Paul. Those traveling together consisted of a military unit under the command of Julius, a centurion of the Augustan Cohort (Acts 27:1), a contingent of prisoners (Acts 27:42), of which Paul was one, Paul's traveling companions, Luke and Aristarchus (Acts 28:1, Col. 4:10), and a sizable company of Christians from Rome who had traveled out of the city to meet Paul and accompany him on the journey in (Acts 28:15).

The uniqueness of Paul lay not in his visage or his origins. Neither would have given a Roman or most others a pause in the midst of a busy day. Neither at this time was Paul worthy of special attention by the proverbial man in the street because of his status or accomplishments. Paul was obviously something of a hero, however, to a very small segment of the populace whom Romans generally placed in the category of one of the near eastern religio-ethnic peoples, more specifically the Jews. Various persons considered them a sect of the Jews (Acts 24:5, 28:22), and perhaps an unusual one at that.

They believed that Jesus, who grew up in Nazareth in Palestine, was the Son of God. Not only that, they asserted that he died for the sins of mankind, and that God raised him from the dead. Because of his death and resurrection, all those who believed he is indeed God's Son will one day live resurrected in the presence of God. These convictions, for the most part, sounded strange to the cosmopolitan ears of Roman citizens.

Paul in Rome

Paul was brought to Rome a prisoner. He was there at his own request. He was first arrested in Jerusalem at the temple, but later taken to Caesarea, the Roman provincial capital on the Mediterranean coast. After two years as a prisoner he requested a hearing before Caesar, the Roman emperor. He may have believed that a decision on his case in Jewish territory would result in condemnation and death. But more pressing was a conviction that if he told the Christ story in Rome and to the emperor it was the same as if the whole empire had heard (Col. 1:23). In Rome Paul was given considerable freedom to tell his story. He was allowed to rent a house and receive guests, constrained only by a soldier who continuously prevented his escape (Acts 28:16,30). We are told that Paul stayed in Rome under those circumstances for two whole years (Acts 28:30). What happened after that is unclear though various suggestions persist.

Paul's Message

Paul was a different, but intriguing figure in Rome. At that stage his conviction that his work would effect a profound change in the empire seemed just a dream. Two centuries later, however, it was indeed a reality. If nothing else can be stated about Paul it must be said he was a true believer. He believed, according to what he had already written to the Roman Christians, that Jesus is Lord, that is, he is identified with God who created the heaven and the earth (Rom. 10:9, 1:20). He is in fact the Son of God who died, but whom God raised from the dead (Rom. 1:3,4). He died for the sins of those who believe so they may be accepted by God (Rom. 4:25). He was raised by God for the justification of believers so they may live with him now and forever in the age beyond (Rom. 6:8). Because Paul believed that God entered human history and will dramatically change those humans who will accept his Son, he saw a turn in history. A new and growing body of people will hear the proclamation of good news (Rom. 10:14,15). They will be a righteous people acceptable to God (Rom. 1:17), forgiven of sin through the death of the Son, and empowered to a God chosen life through the inner presence of the Holy Spirit (Rom. 8:9). They will be from all peoples, not just God's age old people, the Jews (Rom. 9:24). This will be a growing body. They will be preserved and protected by God through all future disasters and from the actions of evil powers, whatever their origin (Rom. 8:37-39). The work of God through his Son is powerfully reconstructing human history for a count-down when God will bring it to an end. And not only will human history come to an end, but creation itself as it now exists (Rom. 8:22-25).

Paul's views, if true, threatened the Roman Empire at its very core. He had accepted these new convictions thirty years before in distant Damascus. He declared to all comers the conviction that Jesus is Son of God. Commencing in Syria, he worked his way across Asia Minor, then into Greece, and now he declared the same point of view in Rome itself, the capital of the empire. In his travelings and pleadings, he left a wake of believers across the empire.

Paul as a Church Planter and Cultivator

Paul's contribution to the change in history was not just a set of convictions about God's work and the future of humanity. He did not simply convert persons to a different outlook on reality, then move on. He was convinced that God's work called for a new kind of human. In his vision this ideal human lived morally and ethically according to the demands of God. Not only did the Holy Spirit empower this new man, but such persons would encourage one another through meeting together and sharing the love of Christ (Rom. 12:3-13). Wherever Paul went he demanded that the believers come together periodically and especially on the first day of the week, the day on which Jesus rose from the dead (1 Cor. 16:2). Through this means believers, regardless of background would be molded into a new loving and caring people (Gal. 3:27).

Perhaps Paul's significance lay in the fact that he gathered believers in Christ together in bodies which he called churches (Rom. 16:1-16). Paul was a church planter. He planted churches where none existed before. He considered church planting as the heart of his work (1 Cor. 3:6, Rom. 15:20-24).

Not only did Paul plant churches, he nourished them. He stayed with the new believers until they passed through their first crisis of persecution (1 Thess. 2:14). He got to know them intimately. He helped them work through the implications of accepting Christ by untiring personal instruction and relationship (1 Thess. 2:7-12). As permitted, he visited and revisited to encourage and further instruct believers in the faith (1 Cor. 16:5-11). He sent fellow workers if he could not come himself (2 Cor. 7:5-7). When he could do neither, he wrote letters. These letters were to enhance faith, explain disputed points, exhort to unity and faithfulness, and encourage growth in Christ. Paul kept up with his churches. He cared. He taught them to care. The result was that he founded dozens of churches with which he was periodically in touch. He knew the temperature of their faith. He knew when problems arose. He knew when they reverted to or adapted views of reality from the culture in which they had grown up and in which they now found themselves.

The Setting for Ephesians and Colossians

Ephesians and Colossians may be properly studied together since they are from the same period in Paul's ministry. According to the best traditional judgment they were both written during Paul's imprisonment in Rome. That is the reason we took up the life of Paul as he entered Rome. We are simply told in these epistles that Paul is in prison (Eph. 3:1, 4:1; Col. 4:3). Scholars argue endlessly about possibilities other than Rome. Some entertain an Ephesian imprisonment, which may or may not have happened. Others argue that Paul wrote letters from Caesarea while he was there. But there are, despite scholarly reservations, solid reasons for the traditional Roman provenance.

Despite being imprisoned in Rome, Paul was exhilarated by the opportunities and the successes of his preaching. In Colossians Paul writes "All over the world this gospel is producing fruit and growing" (Col. 1:6). In the Philippian letter, also written from Rome, perhaps the earliest of the four prison epistles, which also include Philemon, Paul writes even more specifically. "Now I want you to know, brothers, that what has happened to me has really served to advance the gospel. As a result, it has become clear throughout the whole palace guard and to everyone else that I am in chains for Christ. Because of my chains, most of the brothers in the Lord have been encouraged to speak the word of God more courageously and fearlessly" (Phil. 1:12-14). If one continues to read in Philippians 1 he picks up even more on Paul's mood of praise and rejoicing, confident that God is using him to bring his long range plans to fruition.

Paul's expansive and optimistic mood is important for understanding Ephesians and Colossians. In both of these letters Paul addressed the larger implications for the work of Christ for universal history. So confident was he of the manner in which Christianity was making headway in the world that he spoke freely of the cosmic consequences of the death of Christ. In these two letters Paul is not so concerned to address specific problems of new churches as he does in Galatians and 1 Corinthians.

The Situation to Which the Letters Were Addressed

Every communication has two basic components, a sender and a recipient. To understand a communication we need to know something about the sender and his circumstances and the recipient and his. We have written in some detail about Paul the sender. Now we turn to the recipients. Here we will make certain general observations since detailed observations will follow as we take up each letter.

Geographical Setting

The Colossian letter was addressed to Christians in the city of Colossae in western Asia Minor. Colossae was located on the Lycus River eighty miles east and a bit south of Ephesus. It was an important trading center at one time, but had declined by the first century. The question arises with the Ephesian letter as to whom the recipients actually were. Most translations these days either leave "Ephesus" out in Ephesians 1:1 or explain in a footnote, "Some early manuscripts do not have *in Ephesus.*" A reason for thinking the letter was not intended alone for Ephesus is 1:15 in which Paul says "ever since I heard about your faith," as if he did not have firsthand acquaintance with the recipients. It is my view, as explained in the next chapter, that Paul wrote the letter for circulating to all the churches in western Asia Minor, seven of which are mentioned in Revelation 2, 3. If so, the geographical setting for Ephesians is much the same as that of Colossae.

Paul's Connection

Paul arrived in Ephesus in A.D. 53 for an extended stay of three years. His converts included not only residents of the city, but also those from surrounding towns who came in for trade and commerce. One of Paul's strategies in church planting was to establish a church in a major trade center in expectation that converts from the interior towns would return home and themselves plant churches. We know, for example, that the church at Colossae was planted by Epaphras, a native of that city and probably converted by Paul in Ephesus (Col. 1:7). We have already mentioned Paul's intensive interest in the churches he himself planted. In Colossians and Ephesians we become aware that he likewise felt a unique caring relationship with churches planted by his converts. Not only did he send letters, he dispatched various persons to them, associated with him in his ministry (Col. 4:7-18).

The People

The religious influences in western Asia Minor were various. The old native religions involving contradictory actions of the various gods and animal sacrifices were overlaid in some cases with Egyptian, Eastern, and mystery religions. The neighboring city to Colossae, Hierapolis, possessed a famous shrine to the goddess Cybele. There was a sizable Jewish population in the region. Two thousand Jews, imported from Mesopotamia and Babylon, settled there about two hundred years earlier. A century prior to Paul, temple taxes sent to Jerusalem indicate approximately 11,000 adult Jewish males. From various Jewish sources it is clear that Judaism had accommodated to the native religions. The Judaism from which early Christian converts were won in western Asia Minor represented an essentially syncretistic Judaism. Some strains were on the way to what in the second century is labeled Gnosticism. To understand the nature and message of Colossians and Ephesians an explanation of these outlooks is necessary.

Ephesians and Colossians are exciting letters. They exhibit the utter confidence of Paul that through the death of His Son, God is pushing back darkness and evil in all regions of the universe. Christians are therefore called upon to center life in Christ so they may mature and grow upward in him as head of the body, the church. In this manner they participate in the exciting and glorious work of God as he reclaims the universe for Himself.

Questions—Chapter 1

1. Why is it impcrtant to know something about Paul in Rome in order to understand Ephesians and Colossians?

2. What was distinctive about Paul as a person?

3. How would Paul's message have been viewed by the average person in the Roman empire?

4. What were Paul's chief contributions to the early church?

5. What can you say about the geography, people, and religion of the region to which these letters were written?

Chapter 2

EPHESIANS: THE CHARACTER, THE SITUATION, THE MESSAGE

Most of Paul's letters commence by addressing persons, then specific problems in which persons are involved. Ephesians is an exception. This letter begins in an attitude of praise and anticipation. Paul is overwhelmed by God's age old plans and their ultimate execution through the death and resurrection of Jesus right in his own life time. He is awed that his own life and ministry play a vital role in these unprecedented developments. Through the first half of the letter one is impressed with the grandeur of vision, the elevated style, and the aura of praise.

The Character

Various persons have noted that Ephesians is not a letter in the usual sense. It might better be described as a theological homily or discourse or extended prayer. Some have proposed that it was designed to be read at baptismal occasions. Each of these perspectives are suggestive. The letter is basically a reflection on God's work through Christ in the universe, and a translation of that work concretely into family and occupational life. One finds throughout the letter Paul's prayer vocabulary. In Chapter 1 he speaks of praise, thanksgiving, and intercession. It is likewise true that reading the document at a baptismal ceremony would make sense. But despite the insightfulness in these observations, Ephesians seems best described as a sermon divided into two parts: (1) doctrine, chapters 1-3, and (2) application, chapters 4-6.

In view of the character of the document, it seems best to

think of it as prepared by Paul specifically for the purpose of circulating to the churches planted by his converts in the region around Ephesus. We know that Paul wrote letters which he felt would be of value to more than one church (Col. 4:16). The matters Paul addressed, for example, Christians on the verge of forgetting about their Old Testament roots, and deference to the various heavenly powers were common to the region. If the letter is intended for several churches, we have an explanation why Paul was not personally acquainted with many of the recipients (1:15, 3:2,3, 4:21) and why the approach and style differ from Paul's other letters. The fact that the letter was later identified with Ephesus is also explained. (Recall that *Ephesus* is not found in the better texts in 1:1.) Since it was prepared to circulate to the churches around Ephesus, it took its name from the church which spawned the rest.

A circulating letter-sermon also explains why Ephesians differs from other Pauline epistles. For a century and a half critical scholars have rejected Pauline authorship of Ephesians and the number increases. Ephesians obviously is different from other letters of Paul. That we cannot deny. But the difference can be explained if it is to many churches, not just one; to a region which prefers an elevated and extended style; and by a person who concludes that his arrival in Rome signals the fruition of a life time of effort. Paul's mood would be one of praise, confidence and exaltation. He now would visualize the growing colonies of believers, that is, the church, from an exalted and sublime perspective.

The Situation

Paul, in order to maintain contact with the west Asian churches, corresponded. At least three letters are preserved: Ephesians, Colossians, and Philemon. We cannot establish with any certainty which may have been first. Philemon is addressed to a specific situation having to do with a slave converted in Rome from either Colossae or Laodicea. Colossians reacts to spurious attitudes and practices which threaten the church in that city. Ephesians, as we have argued, addresses the problems more common to a region. My assumption is that Colossians and Ephesians were written about the same time. In fact, they may have both been carried by Tychicus on a single trip from Rome to Asia Minor. Tychicus was originally from the Ephesian region and may have been a convert of Paul's at Ephesus (Acts 20:4). He not only delivered the letters, but was expected to supply detailed information about Paul's well being and success (Eph. 6:21, Col. 4:7).

Concrete theological problems addressed in Ephesians are not immediately obvious. If, however, one notes carefully the matters taken up a pattern emerges. In chapter one God himself is declared to determine the outcome of history which he has accomplished even on earth through the death of his Son. The Son is thereupon head of an earthly body of people, the church. In the second chapter the church has such a unique relationship with God through Christ that it is said to be in the heavenly regions (2:6). Powers other than God are real, but pale in achievement when compared with Christ (1:21). The tendency is for these believers to cut adrift from their Jewish roots for the church (3:6). The need is seen to emphasize the oneness of God and believers (4:1-5). Charges to live a God-like ethical and moral life are offered in chapter 4 and 5 with the challenge to ground these in the cross of Christ. In chapter 6 the other powers are again mentioned, but the armor provided by God through Christ is declared more than adequate to withstand whatever force they may possess.

It is my supposition that Paul was in fact addressing a manner of thinking he knew to be present in western Asia Minor. That was his customary *modus operandi.* The only difference between this and others of Paul's letters is that here he is reacting to a world view of a region rather than specific nuances of it in a given church or locality. It has often been observed that Colossians and Ephesians are much alike. That is the case, I believe, because the problems at Colossae are a sub-set, a local manifestation, of the outlooks of a region. In reflecting on the situation behind Ephesians we are paving the way for also understanding Colossians. When we get to Colossians we can take up the distinctive syncretisms indigenous to that city.

We might be at a loss to explain or interpret the syndrome Paul confronts in Ephesians were it not for a distinct movement or heresy which surfaced among the churches in the second century. That movement came to be referred to as Gnosticism. I am not of the opinion advanced by the German scholars Bultmann, Schmithals, and their disciples, that the full blown Gnostic systems obvious in the second century were already in place in the first or prior to the first century. It is Bultmann's position that early Christianity was in fact a wedding of Jewish apocalypticism and Gnosticism. But I do think that seeds of what in the second century turned out to be Gnosticism were already present in Christian contexts in the first century. We might therefore best identify the views Paul sought to challenge in Ephesians as "incipient Gnosticism."

Gnosticism

For the reader who is puzzled by this term Gnosticism, we turn now to supply a short historical and systematic perspective.

The actual beginnings of Gnosticism are shrouded in the mists of history. My supposition is that it had no one point of origin as did, for example, the Unification Church of Sun Myung Moon, since in its own tradition no one founder is recognized. Rather, it was a movement generated from various syncretistic soils. It arose in different parts of the empire and later congealed into a recognizable entity. But because of inherent individualism and other-worldliness, Gnostic groups were always loosely structured. It could be that its anti-organizational posture, as much as any other factor, accounts for the fact that Gnosticism never really emerged as a major organized religion.

Traditions from the second century held that Simon the sorcerer of Acts 8, some years after his conversion, departed from the faith and founded Gnosticism. The validity of this tradition, however, may be disputed. If so, Gnosticism would have Samaritan origins. Some think its origins were the wisdom or apocalyptic strands of Judaism. Others a highly syncretized Judaism. Still others argue that the soils of Gnosticism are chiefly Hellenistic, drawing to a degree on the mystery religions. Adolf Harnack, the great German church historian, referred to Gnosticism as an extreme Hellenizing of Christianity. Gnosticsm may have in fact emerged from all these soils. My own supposition is that as it pertains to western Asia Minor, hence pertinent to Ephesians and Colossians, incipient Gnosticism arose through Judaism, first influenced by Iranian religions during the two to three centuries the western Asia Minor Jews lived in Babylon and Persia. When these Jews were re-colonized in Asia Minor, they were influenced by the native religions and later by the Egyptian and mystery religions of various sorts. Certain Jews converted to Christianity retained some of these outlooks. Thus they reconstructed their pre-conversion world-views along distinctive Christian lines. By the second century if not sooner contacts would have occurred with other Gnostic Christian groups. Evidence of Gnostic tendencies in the region comes from Revelation, 1 John and the pastorals. The Nicolaitans mentioned in Revelation were hated by the Ephesian church (Rev. 2:6), but embraced by some at Pergamum (Rev. 2:15). The "Synagogue of Satan" at Philadelphia composed of those who "claim to be Jews though they are not," supports the presence of sycretistic Judaism. The *docetism* opposed in 1 John that Christ did not come in the flesh (1 Jno. 4:2) is another manifestation.

What then were the basic views of the Gnostics? They differed in details from group to group but held certain fundamental outlooks in common. It might be the most helpful if we did these schematically with minimal explanation.

(1) Gnostics held that the ways of God are known only to insiders. That is in fact where the name comes from. "Gnosis" in Greek means wisdom or insight. The way of God must therefore be learned from an insider. It is hence a shared mystery.

(2) Gnostics held that the highest God is transcendent and wholly other. He stands outside of the material world and has no relationship whatever with it.

(3) Several lesser deities exist. The material world was created by a lesser deity. What these deities contrive in the Cosmos is most significant for this and other worlds.

(4) Numerous higher beings, both good and bad, occupy hierarchical spheres of the higher regions. These beings are involved in the divine drama of why the universe and human life is as it is.

(5) A special deity or Son of God was sent to reveal to man

the mysteries of God. In second century Gnostic systems Christ variously filled this role.

(6) Since the high God has nothing whatsoever to do with the world, he cannot be the God of the Jews who is the maker of heaven and earth. Likewise the Son of God could not really live in the flesh or die on the cross.

(7) "Salvation" comes through induction into these higher mysteries as brought by the revealer. When one receives the mystery he no longer psychically lives in the realm of matter and flesh. He already lives the resurrected life (2 Tim. 2:18).

(8) Individual response to the mystery is what is crucial. Group involvement means little.

(9) Since the psychic life supersedes all else, involvements of the human flesh are inconsequential. Standard morals and ethics have little significance. In matters of the flesh one can do essentially what he pleases.

Paul's Message

As can be seen these views undercut basic Christian presuppositions. Paul's response in Ephesians is that there is indeed a mystery, but it pertains to what God has done in Christ in human history. God is not apart from human life and the world. In fact, the crucial event for the whole cosmos and man did not take place beyond history as the Gnostics assumed, but in history in the very death of Jesus Christ, Son of God. Whatever other powers there may be, Jesus through his death radically changed their position before God. Jesus is the center of the salvation drama. His death in the flesh made possible the forgiveness of sins and eternal life. The Holy Spirit assures that man is a part of the divine drama. The one who believes does not now live beyond the flesh. He is involved in constant struggle with the evil forces of the universe. But he is protected by the armor of God, Christ and the Holy Spirit. Sin is real and must be battled. Salvation is of the total man, not just the psychic. The material universe and bodily man is as much from God as is the soul or spirit. God's work for a unified cosmos also has to do with how man treats his fellow in the flesh. The church, that is, corporate religious effort, is thus imperative in God's herculean task of reclaiming the universe.

For Paul the Judaeo-Christian view does not divorce God from the material world and history but locates his work precisely in it. Because of the success of God's work in the world and in the church, by the time Paul reaches Rome, he is convinced that God indeed struggles in history and it is there that one looks for manifestations of his action, not beyond history in the cosmos as thought by the Gnostics. To be in the heavenly realms for Paul is not to be situated outside of history, but under the rule of God in history. Paul's confrontation with incipient Gnostics in western Asia Minor is therefore a matter of life and death for the basic premises of Christianity. Paul's message is obviously relevant today. From various twentieth century fronts the significance of the work of God in human history is being eroded. It could be that even we don't comprehend the real battle because we don't fully appreciate how radically Paul makes the death and resurrection of Christ the focal point through which God turned around the course of this universe.

Questions—Chapter 2

1. Is Ephesians an epistle or letter? How can it best be described?
2. To whom was Ephesians written?
3. What was Paul's relationship to the recipients?
4. What were the religious problems addressed in Ephesians?
5. What do you know about Gnosticism in its origins and point of view?
6. What was Paul's manner of responding to these people?

Chapter 3

GOD'S LONG RANGE PLANS (Ephesians 1)

We have now discussed who wrote Ephesians and why. We have also reflected on the recipients of the letter and why they needed what they got. It is time then to add a third dimension to the study. The recipient for a Biblical document is not just those who first received it. Paul speaks of this third dimension when he declared to the Romans concerning the Old Testament, "For everything that was written in the past was written to teach us . . ." (Rom. 15:4). Ephesians was written not just to Ephesians of the first century, but likewise to Ephesians of the twentieth century. By this I mean that certain people today need to hear precisely the same message sent to the original recipients of this letter. That is so because they, or we, have drifted off in the same direction. We can only know when Ephesians speaks to our problems when we have understood their problems. We must now take up these problems concretely, then see how they specifically speak to us in our context.

The Central Message

Already in various ways we have identified the basic message of Ephesians. The first half is doctrinal; the second half practical. Ephesians 5:8-10 does a good job of summing up the two halves. ". . . You are the light in the Lord. Live as children of light . . . and find out what pleases the Lord." Christians are children of light because God has acted through the death of the Son to push back the encroaching darkness. And now because of his "love that surpasses knowledge" (3:19) believers should in awe and gratitude live pleasing to God. Another way to put it is 1:3 in which Paul sets out his purpose.

God "has blessed us in the heavenly realms with every spiritual blessing in Christ."

The impulse and motivation to live God's rules—to do what pleases him, is knowledge of his long range plans for the universe. For Paul, when you get to thinking about these plans and how they are brought to fruition in the death of Jesus you simply have to break out in praise. "Praise be to the God and Father of our Lord Jesus Christ . . ." (1:3). In the outlook of Paul, excitement about the Lord and doing his work is generated by a knowledge of what God has done. He is convinced that if theology precedes, action soon follows. Here we have something to learn from Paul. We think enthusiasm generates itself. If we want to get the church off the pews and into the community we import a "fireball" from another city who is on fire for the Lord. We think what he has will rub off. In fact, it does, for about three weeks. After that we sit and wonder what happened to all the enthusiasm. Paul thinks that first we must be overjoyed and awed by God's limitless care and action on our behalf. Then we will be enthused and motivated for Him.

The Long Range Vision of God (1:1-10)

For Paul the work of God in the universe is dramatic and electric. It is not as with those critics in 2 Peter who scoffed saying "Everything goes on as it has since the beginning of creation" (2 Pet. 3:4). Paul agreed with those who wanted to construct stories about the decisions and plans of the various heavenly powers. But there was a difference. For Paul the good news was that the crucial event took place on the earth itself, not in the realms beyond, and it was the work of one divine being, that is Jesus, Son of God. The other beings, whatever they are, have either an adversary role, or such an insignificant function by way of comparison as to not be worth mentioning. So Paul says that God has "blessed us in the heavenly realms with every spiritual blessing in Christ" (1:3). The heavenly powers which bless man's life have one source—Christ. Furthermore, the source of that power is something which took place on earth. "In him we have redemption through his blood, the forgiveness of sins" (1:7).

What amazed Paul and caused him to break out in praise

was the fact that God had put his plans to make man holy and blameless through Christ on the drawing boards even before he created the world (1:4). This action of God was more than an after thought. Through it God moved according to a plan. The great cause for amazement was that the crucial event in that plan, that is, the death and resurrection of Christ (1:20), took place right there in Paul's generation. That was the critical moment toward which God, creation, and man was moving, ". . . which he purposed in Christ, to be put into effect when the times will have reached their fulfillment" (1:10).

The question is, why did God draw up these amazing plans and execute them, and what are the ramifications? Paul's answer is "In love he predestined us . . ." (1:4,5). This universe and human life are not a quirk—a happenstance. Life is more than the ennui of one meaningless event after another with no purpose anywhere in sight. Amazingly, human life fits into the goals of the universe. The life of man has something to do with why the universe exists to begin with. And all this is so because the God who created the world and man is a God who loves. He is concerned about all he has made. Most of all he is concerned about man made in his image. Human life is not irrational, impersonal, cold, and carried out in an indifferent universe. It is planned. It is headed in a direction. It is all adding up. The God who made the world and man is a loving God. When one goes with him life has direction and meaning. It is warm and loving. Another way of referring to God's love is to talk about his grace (1:6,7), a manifestation of his pleasure and will. It pleases God to be giving and forgiving. It pleases him to plan good things for those who neither merit nor deserve such goodness. It pleases him to surprise his creatures with gifts they cannot anticipate. That is his love. That is his grace. It is an amazing world in which we live because it is God's pleasure to bestow gifts even beyond our comprehension.

A term which Paul employs to identify the long range planning of God is "predestined" (1:5,11). The Greek word so translated means to appoint or decide what to do long in advance. God determined from time immemorial to redeem man from his sin (1:7). Paul put it, "For he chose us in him before the creation of the world." Clearly God is conceived as working out human history from the vantage point of advanced planning (1:11). That God does so is both to man's amazement and consternation. It is to his consternation for thereby human freedom seems negated. Is man simply a puppet for a God who pulls the strings at his good pleasure?

Through the death of his Son God put his plan in place, the plan which preceded the existence of man. But man is free as he stands before that plan. He has the freedom to be a part of it or not. "And you also were included in Christ when you heard the word of truth, the gospel of your salvation. Having believed . . ." (1:13). No one is automatically included in the grace which God has predestined. One is included because he has heard the plan and believed. Man reaches out and receives the gift of God. He may accept it or reject it. True, man is totally dependent on God for God himself to open the door whereby he is accepted. Man cannot manufacture his own salvation. But he is free to receive God's magnanimity or to reject it. The federal government has predestined through legislation that those who arrange energy saving options in their homes may deduct up to seventy percent of the costs from their income tax. That option is available to the home owner. He is not a puppet in the hands of the federal government. He must apply for the deduction in order to receive it. The benefit is not forced upon him. God's great plans and execution only turn around the life of those who with open arms receive his good gifts. He does not presume upon anyone.

Not only does Jesus the Son have a role in the long range plans of God but likewise the Holy Spirit. How does one know, once he believes, that he is a part of God's long range work in history? Paul's answer is that the Holy Spirit is the guarantee. The one who accepts the grace of God is sealed by the Holy Spirit. The believer knows that seal, not as some great, inexplicable surge of emotion, but through the fruit of the Spirit, obvious in "good works, which God prepared in advance for us to do" (2:10). The Spirit attaches our consignment instructions. We are consigned to share his gifts now, but Paul makes it clear that our ultimate destiny is a future inheritance (1:14). Because of the presence of the Spirit we already know something about that inheritance. Some wealthy parents, because of the tax advantages, make sizable gifts to their children while they are still alive. These children receive advance insight as to what awaits them at their parent's death. So the Holy Spirit through current gifts shows who belongs to

God, and in advance, however inadequately, what immeasurable inheritance awaits the believer.

The Other Powers in the Universe

God's long range plans not only encompass man and earth, but everything. ". . . to bring all things in heaven and on earth together under one head, even Christ" (1:10). The implications are not simply for earthly rulers and authorities, but those even beyond the earth (1:21). It is amazing when you stop to think about it. The crucial events in the divine drama all took place on earth. Jesus died on earth (1:7). He was raised by God from the dead on earth (1:20). The Holy Spirit comes to dwell in man on earth (1:13, 2:22). The body of Christ, the church, through which God is bringing his work to fruition is on earth (1:22,23). Right on earth in Paul's time and in our time God is working out his will in such a manner that the ramifications reach as much into heaven as earth. How is that possible, and how are we to understand the heavenly aspects?

To obtain insight we turn to Paul's word *epouranios* (Greek), translated "heavenly places" (RSV, KJV), "heavenly realms" (NIV). Literally the Greek word means "with reference to heaven." While that helps, we do not know how Paul conceives heaven. The meanings of words only to a degree live in dictionaries. They live rather in the discourses of people. In Ephesians Paul employs *epouranios* five times: 1:3,20, 2:6, 3:10, and 6:12. What can we learn of Paul's vision of the "heavenly realms" from these five contexts?

In Ephesians 1:3 Paul says we are "blessed in the heavenly realms." Does this mean we are in the heavenly realms? We commonly presume not. It could mean rather that our blessings are manufactured in the heavenly realms and distributed to us on earth. The problem is that for Paul, the dramatic work of God on our behalf took place on earth. In 1:20 Christ is seated at the right hand of God in the heavenly realm and is far above all the powers. What amazes us, however, is that Christians are raised up with Christ (2:6) and are seated in the heavenly realms with Christ Jesus. The presence of Christians in the heavenly realms is not future but now. This clues us to the fact that Paul must be using "heavenly realm" in some special sense. Not only are Christ and believers in heavenly realms, but also rulers and authorities. Are these earthly authorities? They could be. But in 6:12 we learn that certain evil spiritual beings—rulers, authorities, and powers, who are not flesh and blood inhabit the heavenly realms. What are we to make of all this? What sort of a universe is it Paul posits?

The best answer seems to be that by heavenly realms Paul has in mind not a space or region, but a rule or influence. We tend to think that most things happen because of our boss, our spouse, the kids, our parents, the neighbors, or the government. Paul is of a different opinion. He believes that intermingled with human forces are those which transcend flesh and blood, both good and evil. In Ephesians the good powers are God, Christ, and the Holy Spirit. The evil powers are "the ruler of the kingdom of the air" (2:2), and "rulers, authorities, powers" (6:12). From medieval thought, or John Milton, we think heaven is above, earth is in between, and hell beneath. God stays in heaven, we stay on earth, Satan and his servants stay in hell. Notice that for Paul the chief evil power is the "ruler of the kingdom of the air." (Compare with Job 1:6 in which Satan shows up with the angels before God.) By "heavenly realm" therefore Paul has in mind a rule or power not a region. Christians are in the heavenly realm of God because they are living in the rule, the power of God, Christ, and the Holy Spirit. There is also a rule of the dark powers which is a heavenly realm, but not the realm of God. In any city there are those in control—the insiders. There are also those who have little power—the outsiders. Inside and outside is not a geographical region. The insiders and outsiders may be grouped to some degree, but likely will be distributed throughout the city. The heavenly realm therefore is not a region. It exists wherever power and authority exist whether of evil or good. What Paul means when he says that Christ is "far above all rule and authority, power and dominion" is not to locate him spatially, but to situate his rule in the universe. Upon his death and resurrection the power and authority of Christ in the universe far exceeded that of any other being other than God himself. Whatever other powers mixed up Christians in western Asia Minor revere, they pale in comparison with Christ. If one wears his Christian armor he need not show obeisance to nor fear any other (6:11).

The work of God in the death and resurrection of Christ

therefore is the turning point in history. By that work God circumscribed the forces of evil. Not only that, but as the church grows it will continually erode the influence of evil agents. In Christ, God brought "all things in heaven and on earth together under one head, even Christ" (1:10). "God placed all things under his feet and appointed him to be head over everything for the church" (1:22). "Praise be to the God and Father of our Lord Jesus Christ, who has blessed us in the heavenly realms with every spiritual blessing in Christ" (1:3).

We live in a time in which powers of all sorts demand our attention. The age old "science" of astrology has once again reared its hoary head. Millions read their horoscopes in daily columns. Psychics are consulted by movie magnates, business executives, and police departments. Persons are seduced by fads, movements, and the occult. We are leaned on by politicians, salespersons, and promoters of how-to-do-it. Our world is obviously inhabited by wondrous and demanding forces. The good news offered by Paul is that only one power matters. He is Jesus the Lord who is far above "all rule and authority, power and dominion" (1:21). Whatever these other powers, we need not bother. Our lives are ruled by the one whose power far exceeds what any agent can muster, regardless.

Questions—Chapter 3

1. What is the central message of Ephesians?

2. Does a deeper insight into what God is doing in the world help create enthusiasm in church members?

3. What does Paul envision as the long range plans of God?

4. What does Paul mean by "predestination"?

5. What are the implications of Christ's death for the universe?

6. What is meant by "heavenly realm" in Ephesians?

Chapter 4

THE ONENESS OF HUMANKIND (Ephesians 2:1-3:21)

Paul was convinced that through Christ God hewed out a new man. That man was not a lone individual, herculean like, challenging the powers of the universe. Rather he was part of a corporate body, maturing and growing under, and up to the headship of Christ (1:22, 4:15). This corporate entity, pushing back, encroaching upon, replacing evil in the universe, is the church, the body of Christ of which he is the head. That body is empowered by the Holy Spirit. "In him the whole building is joined together and rises to become a holy temple in the Lord. And in him you too are being built together to become a dwelling in which God lives by his Spirit" (2:21,22).

The long range plans of God were brought to fruition by the death and resurrection of Christ. God did his mighty work in the Son so he could reclaim everything in the universe to himself. Everything in the universe is to be united in Christ (1:10). The unity in Christ is to penetrate every aspect of the universe. He is designated to unify beings in heaven and on earth (1:10). He is to unify ethnic groups separated by hostilities (2:13-16). He is to unify believers in the body (4:2,3). In Jesus Christ, an ever expanding, ever growing body pushes aside whatever is hostile and foreign to God.

In Ephesians 2, 3, Paul sets out God's long range plans for unifying Jew and Gentile in the body of Christ.

One New Man Out of Two

In chapter 2, Paul is concerned about hostilities which persist between Gentiles and Jews. God through the death of his Son arranged the demolition of that iron curtain. In the church, the body of Christ, there are no longer two ethnic groups. God has made one new man out of Jews and Gentiles (2:15). Where hostilities continue, the long range plans of God disintegrate.

The situation to which Paul speaks in Ephesians is the reverse of that found in Galatians. In the Galatian letter Paul confronted converted Jews who "put the squeeze" on Gentile believers to circumcise their sons, observe the sabbath, passover, and other feasts (Gal. 4:10, 5:2). In the Galatian churches it was Jewish Christians who subverted God's preexistent plans to unify humankind. This situation reversed itself a decade later in western Asia Minor. The Christians to whom Ephesians was written apparently were all of Gentile origin (2:1,2,11). There is no mention of a reversion to Jewish customs, forcibly or otherwise. The ties with Judaism are about to become a forgotten memory. These Christians are on the verge of cutting adrift completely from their Jewish roots, perhaps even to deny them. In Paul's view that is to make the Christian faith ahistorical, to reject history as the arena in which God does his important work. The later Gnostics moved in that direction. For them the drama of salvation all took place beyond history. To experience salvation was to be caught up out of history. The God of the Jews was an inferior God because he was the creator of the heaven and earth. The Christ of the naive Christians was completely unsatisfactory. The Gnostic Christ neither lived nor died in the flesh.

Paul feels compelled to remind these Christians of the historic roots out of which they came. Israel was God's people long before the Christians came on the scene. They played a prior role and a significant one in the preexistent plans of God. At that time Gentiles were cut off from the arena of God's work. "Remember that at that time you were separate from Christ, excluded from citizenship in Israel and foreigners to the covenants of the promise, without hope and without God in the world" (2:12). The new man in Christ does not cut adrift from God's relationships with Israel. All that is now a part of his own heritage. Now he incorporates that work into his own self-identity so that it becomes his legacy as well as that of the Jews. "This mystery is that through the gospel the Gentiles are heirs together with Israel, members together of one body, and sharers together in the promise in Christ Jesus" (3:6).

It was Paul's great vision that through Christ God created a new man not with two histories, but one; not with two identities, but one. First Paul showed how the circumstances of all peoples are the same regardless of background. The Gentiles were dead in sin through following the ruler of the kingdom of the air (2:1,2). The Jews likewise were disobedient (2:3). In the past of both lies sin. But because both believe in Christ they are no longer sinners. God through his grace in the resurrection of Christ brought both from death to life (2:4-10). They were saved, that is new men, not through their own efforts, but by the work of God in Christ. Once raised up with Christ both produced a record of Christian deeds as God likewise intended from before the creation of the world (2:10). Obviously, that was the end `of the common heritage since the Jews had numerous documents of formal ties with God which were not available to the Gentiles. But Paul contends that through God's action in Christ, the names of the Gentiles now appear on all these formal documents. "But now in Christ Jesus you who once were far away have been brought near through the blood of Christ" (2:13).

Because of the blood of Christ this two track heritage has been absorbed into one. Neither track in Christ can deny the other. Christ demolished the wall that separates. He ended the name calling and animosity which in the past floated over the wall in both directions (2:14). He accomplished this by "abolishing in his flesh the law with its commandments and regulations" (2:15). Those with reservations about Jewish regulations for Paul are correct. But the way around the law is not to spiritualize, ignore or denounce. God took care of the divisiveness of the law by an event on earth, the fleshly death of the Son. The commandments and regulations at stake in this passage are those which separated Jew from Gentile. The apostles and elders in Jerusalem decreed that the common heritage of Jew and Gentile Christians would not involve circumcision or the various feasts. They were all, however to observe certain items in the law, "You are to abstain from food sacrificed to idols, from blood, from the meat of strangled animals and from sexual immorality" (Acts 15:29). Paul did not reject the common commandments (1 Cor. 7:19) only those which separated men in Christ. The items therefore in Judaism claimed as necessary for a relationship with God which were not bound on Gentiles, Christ abolished by his death. In that manner the self identity of Jew and Gentile in Christ was identical. Christ preached peace (in Hebrew "shalom"—the manner in which one Jew greeted another) to those far away (that is, in rabbinic language, Gentiles) and those near (or the Jews). The greeting to both Jew and Gentile is the same "Peace." Both are thus accepted! (2:17).

Because of the work of Christ, Jews and Gentiles pick up a new identity at the same place. They both share the mighty acts of God from creation on. They likewise share the added foundation of "the apostles and prophets, with Christ Jesus himself as the chief cornerstone" (2:20, also 3:5). Jews and Gentiles have the same heritage, the same legacy, they belong to the same family (3:14,15). All these amazing changes God effects through his Son, and through his Holy Spirit who is at work in the church (3:16-21). What seems impossible to believers, the overcoming of age old hostilities God has, and is accomplishing. He "is able to do immeasurably more than all we ask or imagine, according to his power that is at work within us" (Eph. 3:20). Humans say, "People can never be one. God's dream will never be realized." God says, "If you let me help you, I will see that we realize it."

Mystery, Revelation, Knowledge

You may be puzzled as to why Paul keeps talking about the mystery. What are we to make of this? Is this word some sort of a flag, warning us we have to gear up to search for a hidden insight which isn't immediately obvious? The word mystery clusters in chapter 3 (3,4,9). It is also found in 1:9, 5:22, and 6:19. Other words in the same context (3:2-12) which bear noting are "make known," "wisdom," "revelation," "revealed," and "insight."

If you examine these passages you discover that Paul is presenting the "mystery" in the letter itself. We are not to suppose that we must search farther. If we understand what Paul is saying in Ephesians we understand the mystery. The mystery is that before the worlds were created God planned to reconcile everything in the universe to himself through the death and resurrection of Christ and in the church. In chapter 3 the particular emphasis is on how God in these projections even included the reconciling of Jew and Gentile (3:6). One reason Paul refers to these plans of God as mystery is that the complete story was not available to man until disclosed in the time of Christ. "In reading this, then, you will be able to understand my insight into the mystery of Christ, which was not made known to men in other generations as it has now been revealed by the Spirit to God's holy apostles and prophets" (3:4,5 also 3:9).

My supposition is that by using the language singled out: "mystery," "revelation," "knowledge," and so on, Paul attempted to beat those on the way to Gnosticism at their own game. They claim they have a divine drama to relate, available only to those to whom the mystery has been disclosed. Some heavenly being as revealer has conveyed the mystery. Paul thus jumps into the game playing by their rules, that is, their concepts and vocabulary. But in the story he has to tell, his mystery is different. Their story has to do with awesome happenings in the cosmos beyond human existence and history. Paul's story discloses the astonishing plans of God which are conceived in such a way that amazingly the crucial events take place on earth, on the cross, in the resurrection, and in the church. The mystery of which Paul speaks here is the Gospel, the good news of what God has done in Jesus Christ.

Oneness Today

At the end of the last chapter we pointed out that God's work in Christ means that he is the only power or authority we need to listen to in this world or from any realm beyond. In Christ God has unified all power and authority, whether on earth or beyond earth. God has centered all power and authority in him so as to accomplish his program of a growing united body under the headship of Christ. To attain this oneness on earth God sets out to draw persons of all ethnic backgrounds into the church. What ramifications does this have for us in the twentieth century?

First, our identity in Christ involves the work of God from creation. Our heritage is the same as that of Israel. We, much as the people to whom Ephesians is written are in trouble if we cut adrift from the Old Testament. The Old Testament, in the actions of God and the reasons for them, is in fact our roots. Christ has replaced by his work the ceremonies and institutions of the Old Testament. But a God who acts in history is not thereby overthrown. Marcion, a second century churchman, tainted with at least Gnostic like tendencies, sought to cut Christians adrift from the Old Testament. The outcome was a religion without historical roots. In our own time various moves within Christianity also try to construct a religion situated beyond time and history. Liberal movements respond to pressures for universalism and transcendentalism. In these circles, a religion is said to be true if its presuppositions have to do with what is beyond time and space. What happens in history is an embarrassment. Historical events have to be "demythologized." Then in conservative circles, emphasis on mountain peak experiences with God tends to defuse the significance of what God has accomplished in the past. What counts is what God did for me this morning. The God of Abraham, Isaac, Jacob, and our Lord Jesus Christ is somehow lost in the fogs of "my" God.

Second, if we are a part of the grand work of God, our churches must strive to incorporate persons from all racial and ethnic backgrounds. This is not to claim that a church must suffer guilt if it fails to include all the possible races. Obviously no one church in the New Testament period had every race. But we are to receive and work among all the races as much as we are able. Likewise we are not to forget our historic ties with Judaism. God has not turned his back on his people of old. He still yet struggles to incorporate them into the church, the body of the Son. They do not need to reject their Jewishness. They need rather to accept Jesus as Messiah, and Christians as their brothers in the Lord.

Third, I'm convinced from this fresh study of Ephesians that my own vision of the work of God in Christ has been limited in the past. The action of God in the death and resurrection of Jesus Christ has more far-reaching consequences than I had ever imagined. It reaches not only into the life of man, but life throughout the universe. Furthermore, the work God is doing through his church defies the imagination. God is uniting humankind in the church. He is working toward that point at which everything in the universe will be one. And this mind-boggling undertaking goes on in the church. "Now to him who is able to do immeasurably more than all we ask or imagine, according to his power that is at work within us, to him be glory in the church and in Christ Jesus throughout all generations, for ever and ever! Amen."

Questions—Chapter 4

1. Why does Paul think that a main objective of God in the world is unity?
2. In what ways did Christ's death make Jews and Gentiles one?
3. Can Christians cut adrift from the Old Testament?
4. What does Paul mean by "mystery"?
5. Are Christians to see their work today as bringing unity into the world?

Chapter 5

GROWTH INTO MATURE HUMANITY (Ephesians 4:1-32)

With the last chapter we finished the doctrinal part of Ephesians, chapter 1-3. We turn now to the practical implications. Paul himself notes the shift by using *oun,* "therefore" (4:1).

The call of the Christian (4:1), that is, his participation in the magnificent plans of God, elicits his best efforts to be God's kind of person. "I urge you to live a life worthy of the calling you have received" (4:1). If we have been captivated by the mind expanding action of God set forth in Ephesians 1-3, and we have received God's grace so as to be included in his grand family (3:15), we are led to ask the critical question, "How then shall I live?" Paul hopes we are at that point. The rest of Ephesians is an answer to that question.

The Unity of the Spirit

God himself set in motion the means through which the powers beyond will eventually be united through Christ or destroyed. He likewise dissolved the differences between Jew and Gentile. These actions are set out in chapters 1-3. God also set in motion the unity of believers in the church. But in the latter case he is dependent on the help of the body of Christ—the church. The calling of believers, as soon becomes obvious, is to manifest the servanthood to Christ in the church, in the family, and in their occupation, so as to participate with God in bringing all in unity with himself. The call of the believer is urgent and challenging. When we seriously take up the call we enter into partnership with God. In our own unique way we participate in the administration of the mystery "which for ages past was kept hidden in God, who created all things" (3:9). When we take up his work God does not leave us to flounder around. He works in and through us.

In verses 2-6 Paul speaks of the nature of the life, hence unity in Christ, and its basis. What are the traits of those who heal rifts? They are like their Lord who expressed love and concern. He gave. He lived for others, not for himself. Paul says, "Be completely humble and gentle" (4:2). These qualities certainly defuse dissension. My siblings consisted of two brothers and a sister. My mother's parents lived a half mile away. Sometimes we walked down to their place to play. After a time invariably we would get in an argument. We might play Monopoly. As with most kids we couldn't always agree about the rules. My Grandmother, who was never demanding, always giving, hence humble, helpful, gentle and patient, would come around to see what the fuss was all about. She patiently listened to all the views, stopping those who interrupted, and after making sure we all got in our two cents worth told us what the rules were if she knew. If not, she looked them up. If a "fight" broke out again five minutes later she returned and thereafter as many times as need be. By her basic traits she settled numerous antagonisms even though she did not aggressively seek the role of a peacemaker with adults. The new man of God in working for a unified body is "patient, bearing with one another in love" (4:2). The spirit of God is at work in that person as he opens the door for the Spirit. The Spirit does not force his way in. But if permitted to enter he effects unity and joins or bonds believers together in peace. They are healthy and whole, welcomed and accepted. The Spirit works in the believer to effect such unity.

God's aim and effort is to mold the universe into one. He is one, as also everything which follows from him. The Lord—by this designation Paul has in mind Jesus Christ—is one. The work of God which elicits faith is one, therefore one faith. The entry into the body is through baptism—one baptism. The one baptism is of the water and the Spirit (Jno. 3:5). These are one and the same and cannot be separated just as the salvific acts are one. God the Father is one and for that reason wants his world to be one. It is therefore obvious that the way to be worthy of the calling we have received is a herculean effort to be the sort of an individual who will bring about the unity of humankind.

We are not left to our own devices to achieve this great end. God has distributed gifts to assist us in this impossible undertaking. We say, "God, you don't know how hard it is for me to accept everybody and be a peacemaker. I grew up in a large family and I had to fight for everything I had. Or, I was an only child and I am accustomed to doing things myself in my own way. You can't really expect me to be a loving person, God. My parents were in their forties when I was born. They didn't believe in showing affection. We never touched each other. We never used endearing words. God, you know how I was brought up. There's just a lot of people I could never accept. I have never been able to put up with braggarts, loudmouths and persons on an ego trip. I was brought up to distrust fast talking city slickers. I just have a terrible time accepting anyone who is not my kind of person."God says, "I know it. No one is more aware than I of what you are up against. I don't expect you to do this on your own. I will supply gifts to leaders who will help you. I will also award you the gift of service so you can do what otherwise would be impossible."

We need to notice several things about the gifts. First, each believer receives a gift so he can contribute to the total work of the body of Christ (4:7). The word first used is *charis,* translated "grace." This word obviously is the root for *charismata* (Rom. 12:6) translated "gifts." We could literally translate charismata "grace things." What God gives to each believer is not something he has already. Neither is it deserved. He gets it because of God's grace. It is God's gift. You may not be a loving person. You do not deserve the gift of love. But God who is graceful grants you that gift anyway. There is a teaching about, that people without gifts need to seek them. They need to pray and ask others to pray so they might obtain a second blessing. That is a human idea. It is not Paul's. Paul believes that when each person enters the body of Christ God provides a gift or gifts.

Second, the gifts are not identical. Different people have different gifts (4:11). Some churches stress identical obligations for each member. In their thinking the unity of the body depends upon each person doing what everyone else does. Paul does not think unity is based on each member having the same gift, doing the same thing, or being a Xerox copy. Unity comes through serving one Lord, not through identical service.

Third, in this list, the gifts identify offices rather than types of services. Some of these offices continue some do not. God's loving body is not simply a by-product, an after thought or accident. God got it off on the right foot through apostles and prophets. He guided them so as to provide a body of love and unity. But once the foundations were laid these offices did not continue. Through the centuries God continues to guide the body into his channels of unity through evangelists, pastors, and teachers. Notice the job assignment of these officers. They are to "prepare God's people for works of service, so that the body of Christ may be built up" (4:12). Paul does not specify the gifts of service in Ephesians. They are for loving and serving each other in the body of Christ. They enable the free flow of love and goodness in the body. In Romans Paul is more specific: serving, teaching, encouraging, contributing to the needs of others, leadership, and showing mercy (Rom. 12:7,8).

Fourth, these gifts are not for exhibitionism, mountain peak experiences, attention getting, or for the personal pleasure or faith building of those who have them. Rather, they are "body gifts." They are to be employed in and for the body. They are to bring love, maturity, and unity to the body. ". . . until we all reach unity in the faith and in the knowledge of the son of God and become mature, attaining to the whole measure of the fullness of Christ" (4:13).

Because of the work of Christ and the Spirit in the body, the church matures in sharing, loving, and leading the world into unity. The older a church, the more adept it should be at bringing believers into peace, love, service and unity. The ways of infants who are self seeking and attached to any dissenter who comes along will be left behind. Each individual in the body, because of the gift God has given him for service in the body will contribute to the maturing of the body. The body will more and more be ruled by the Lordship of Christ. He will control the body. It will move toward his unity and his love in all its various parts or members. It will be aggressively involved in the age old plans of God to reconcile and unify as much of humankind as will respond to the goodness of God. "Instead, speaking the truth in love, we will in all things grow up into him who is the Head, that is, Christ. From him the whole body, joined and held together by every supporting ligament, grows and builds itself up in love, as each part does its work" (4:15,16).

Negating Love and Unity

It is possible for those who enter the body of Christ to drag their feet and contribute to darkness and disunity. God makes available his help. He does not force it on us. There are other beings at work: rulers, authorities, and powers of this dark world. They divert believers into evil deeds. God created free beings for whom love is possible. A robot can move. A robot can be attracted electronically to another robot. A robot cannot love. It cannot decide to do evil rather than good—to love rather than hate. Since God is love he desires love in return. He therefore created beings who exhibit the characteristics that make love possible, the main one being the freedom to love or not to love. Even certain heavenly beings chose the path of dissension, hatred, and sin (2 Pet. 2:4). They are those dark powers. Men likewise have the choice to pursue darkness. They are not compelled to walk in the light. The dark forces encourage and entice non-believers and believers to go down paths of darkness rather than paths of light. Unwary believers contribute to the disintegration of God's universe, rather than to its unity. So Paul challenges these Christians, "So, I tell you this, and insist on it in the Lord, that you must no longer live as the Gentiles do, in the futility of their thinking. They are darkened in their understanding" (4:17,18).

It is interesting to look at the traits of those who live in darkness. These traits undermine brotherhood and unity, contributing rather to self gratification. "They have given themselves over to sensuality so as to indulge in every kind of impurity, with continual lust for more" (4:19). They are caught up in falsehoods (4:25), they are given over to anger (4:26), and they steal (4:28). All of these actions disrupt human well-being and unity. They create distrust, ill will, harsh words, and anger. They are the ways of the enemy, not the ways of God.

God is at work to bring his world into a loving and sharing relationship. The same disruptive results obtain from unwholesome talk (4:29), bitterness, rage, anger, brawling, slander and malice (4:31).

Walking in the ways of darkness, that is, ways that alienate, disrupt, distort, and destroy, grieve the Holy Spirit. That is so first, because the believer is sealed by the Spirit. A professional football team signs a blue chip college running back. The first season he is rookie of the year. The second he is the league leading ground gainer. The third he wins the trophy as the most valuable player in the Superbowl. The fourth year he gets into drugs, does a sloppy job, is impossible to get along with, and offers to fight the quarterback. He is under contract. He is sealed. But he is worthless to the owner, the coach, and the team. He grieves them all deeply. As it turns out he is contributing more to the success of his opponents than that of his own team. The Holy Spirit is likewise grieved when it turns out that the one he signed is aiding and abetting the powers of darkness who do their best to disrupt and fracture humankind.

We also learn from "grieving the Spirit" that the Spirit does not overpower so as to coerce into his bidding. The Spirit prompts. The Spirit pleads. The Spirit encourages. But the Spirit relies on the believer to avail himself of the power offered. We have within our grasp the ability to contribute in an unprecedented manner to the grand plan of God to unite heaven and earth, Jew and Gentile, man and man. It is up to us. We are not asked to do the impossible. We are asked to open our lives to the Spirit of God and let him do the impossible through us.

Questions—Chapter 5

1. How can we be involved in God's work of unifying people?
2. How do the "gifts" contribute to God's work?
3. What is Paul's view of gifts in Ephesians 4?
4. Contrast the characteristics of those in light and darkness.
5. What do the "seal" of the Spirit and "grieving" the Holy Spirit mean?

Chapter 6

LIVING THE CROSS (Ephesians 5:1-20)

Officials solicit right actions in various ways. Colleges usually have a handbook in which the "dos and don'ts" of campus life are set out. Manufacturing plants have operations manuals which tell the right and wrong ways to get things done. Football teams many times identify desired behavior by naming a player of the week. The player who does best is held up as a model. Sometimes leaders do not set forth specific rules, but offer a principle by which all decisions are to be made and measured. One such rule might be, "When deciding on a course of action recognize that you are not deciding for yourself, but for all mankind."

Now how does Paul go about encouraging people to walk in light rather than darkness (5:8)? He held himself up for a model, as he replicates Christ (1 Cor. 11:1). Paul likewise is not reluctant to lay it on the line with "dos and don'ts." But there is something about Paul's "dos and don'ts." They are not a series of unrelated rules. Paul invariably offers a principle from which the detailed rules originate. In that manner the believer can see the reasons behind the rules and better know how to apply them in specific instances. We have already noticed in chapter 4 that the principle from which Paul weighed specific kinds of behavior was whether it contributed to the unity of humankind.

In the section of Ephesians beginning with 4:32 the controlling factor is the unifying power of the cross. The cross implicates giving and sharing. Christ gave his life in behalf of others. He submitted or subjected himself to others out of love and in order to realize God's powerful vision of united humankind. Giving is the way of the cross. Taking is the road to alienation and separation. So Paul declares as the basic principle from which to decide on human actions. "Submit to one another out of reverence for Christ" (5:21).

Just as in Christ God Forgave You

In the last part of chapter 4 Paul went through a series of actions which constituted the ways of darkness. These were pre-Christian life styles, embittering man against man. Through it a woman became alienated from her neighbor.

But there is another—a God given style for life. God set it out as if on a placard for all to see (Gal. 3:1). He made a public demonstration through the Son. "But when the time had fully come, God sent his Son, born of a woman" (Gal. 4:4). In the Son God said, "If you want to know how to live I have prepared my answer. It is not on the front and back of a flyer. It is not a fifty-four page pamphlet. My answer is a person—my very own Son. If you want to know how to live, look at him. Learn about him. Emulate him. Take up his ways. Follow him." If you want to know what I am like, if you want to know my ways, vigorously search out the Son. "No one has ever seen God, but God the only Son who is at the Father's side, has made him known" (Jno. 1:18).

For Paul, the style of life which is light in the Lord (4:8) does not begin with a set of rules. It begins with a person, the very Son of God. The rules that emerge are gleaned from seeing what he did, learning why he did it, then replicating that way of life in one's own person. In Ephesians 4:32-6:9 the focal point for our model in the action of Christ is his death, the reason why he died, and what he accomplished through it.

The stage is set in 4:32. In contrast with the behavior which brings divisiveness, the way of Christ brings forgiveness, healing and peace. "Be kind and compassionate to one another, forgiving each other, just as in Christ God forgave you." Paul doesn't approach it, "Now the first rule for Christian living is forgiving. So you Christians out there, forgive!" Rather he says that believers are to forgive because in fact, they have already been forgiven. "Just as in Christ God forgave you." What occasion did Paul have in mind in which God forgave us? Obviously, he had in mind the death of the Son. "In him we have redemption through his blood, the forgiveness of sins" (1:7). Paul has earlier emphasized that we are not alone in our effort to bring love and unity in a cruel and contentious world. God does not say, "Here my world. It is up to you. I want you to remold it. I've got other things to do now. But when I get back to you I want to see a completed job." Rather, he rolls up his sleeves and works in and along with the believer through his Holy Spirit.

Furthermore, by his own action he prepares us for the task ahead of time. When he tells us to remake our world by being a forgiving person he himself has prepared us. We know what it is to be a terrible person, messed up in numerous ways, a perpetrator of sinful acts. During those times we wondered how a mother could love us, much less God. We felt so estranged, so far from people and from God. Certainly our actions were so unlike those of God, by his standards we were the scum of the earth. But then we heard the astonishing news. Regardless of how terrible, how messed up, how foreign, God wants us. He wants to include us in. He desires that we be in his in group, in his loving circle. He desires us, not because of anything we have done, but because of what he has done. "But God demonstrates his own love for us in this: While we were still sinners, Christ died for us" (Rom. 5:8). Once we were worthless. But when we reached out and accepted the grand offer of God's forgiveness we were accepted—were affirmed. It wasn't anything we did. "For it is by grace you have been saved, through faith—and this not from yourselves it is the gift of God—not by works, so that no one can boast" (2:8).

Once forgiven—amazing grace!—we are freed to forgive others. "Forgiving each other, just as in Christ God forgave you" (4:32). I look at my world and say, "God's dream of a universe where love, forgiveness and unity prevail is impossible." God says, "Oh no, it isn't. I've already paved the way. I myself, through the decisive act of forgiveness in the death of the Son, have blazed the trail. Now endless pioneers can make their way to new frontiers of love, of caring, of forgiveness." I look around and I see people so different, so foreign. Some are snobs, others dirty and unkempt, and still others secretive and clannish. "Lord, I can't even relate to those people, much less love or forgive them!" He comes back, "Oh yes, you can. You looked worse than that from my perspective. I had no idea how I was going to relate to you. But I did. I did it through my Son and his death! Because I did it for you I have freed you to accept, love, forgive."

And Gave Himself Up for Us

The argument that proper behavior for Christian living takes its beginning with God through the Son continues in 5:1, "Be imitators of God, therefore, as dearly loved children and live a life of love, just as Christ loved us and gave himself up for us as a fragrant offering and sacrifice to God." God wishes his world to be one. The Son set the mode through which oneness is attainable. It is to be attained through love, which is defined not as desire for the other, but as giving up for the other. It is subjecting one's self to the other—submitting to the other. In the verses that follow these words need to be watched: "love," "gave up," "sacrifice," "submit," "subject." These words all point to the same phenomena. These are the governing concepts for Christian living because they represent Christ. In the case of Jesus not only his death, but his life was the way of the cross. In life he submitted to God. He also submitted to people. He lived his life for them. He cared. He hurt. He helped.

Before Paul gets on with ramifications of giving, submission, love, he again addresses negative traits which defy the action of Christ. It is not certain from Ephesians whether the view circulated that if one is saved he is beyond sin in the spirit so whatever his flesh does can be disregarded. It is certain John confronted people who thought that way (1 Jno. 3:4-6). Paul makes it clear, regardless, that sin was taken care of by the blood of Christ. Christ died for sin in the flesh. Paul's first list cites sexual immorality, impurity, and greed (5:3). These are improper for God's holy people. Why? They are improper because they represent taking, demanding, desire. They tear up people rather than bringing them together. They are getting, not giving. Furthermore, obscenity, foolish talk or coarse joking make no contribution to helping, caring, and loving. Many a fight has ensued over obscene, cruel words. The giving, loving nature of Christ, in contrast, brings one to spend spare moments in thanksgiving (5:4). People who live for number one, for what they can take, are not involved in the work of God now. In the future they have no "inheritance in the kingdom of Christ and of God" (5:5). God cannot tolerate people who turn upside down his plans for uniting the universe. To do so would be to toss in the towel. It would be to succumb to a fractured, hurtful, disruptive, deteriorating reality. Such a reality is opposite to that of our God. He is a God of ready forgiveness to those who come over and work on his side. There is no way he can be the kind of God he is, however, and let persons with opposite values than his determine the course of the universe. Because of who he is he obviously doesn't have to bow to these disruptive forces, and he won't. For this reason, believers are to withhold their support. "Therefore do not be partners with them" (5:7).

Those who know what God is attempting for his universe, who have accepted God's gracious offer, need to get on with the task. Because they have inside information about these astonishing plans and achievements they need to get up off their hands and energetically and joyfully bring humankind into a loving relationship with God and their fellows. They need to start giving as he gave! Believers had already flitted away enough talent and energy prior to hearing the good news. It is time now to give it one's best. "Live as children of light" (5:8). Cut adrift from the disruptive evil that thwarts the rule of God! Don't ignore it. Expose it (5:11). It is time to quit dilly dallying. It is time to pull out of the schizophrenia of being attracted to God's magnificent vision, yet at the same time being drawn to immediate desires. Give up the demands of the flesh which tear human life asunder! Pitch in wholeheartedly and unreservedly. Go with God. There is no time to waste. You have already revved up the motor; you have already spun the wheels too long. "Wake up, o sleeper, rise from the dead, and Christ will shine on you" (5:14).

The person who has made the commitment, who has said he will go with the blueprints of God, needs to seriously consider what he is doing with his life. He needs to make the most of every opportunity to exhibit love, submission, reconciliation, and unity (5:16). While the body of God's Son is growing, and God is winning over the world to his ways, sometimes it is two steps forward and one backwards. The powers of evil are sufficient enough of themselves to curtail and disrupt the divine efforts. One cannot flit away the moments. To do so is to aid and abet the enemy. One needs a concerted effort so as to obtain a clear vision of God's work (1:17). One does not have time to get "spaced out" on wine or drugs of any sort. There is too much positive, powerful, loving work to carry out in the world (5:18). One must instead open his life to the prompting of the Spirit. The Spirit pours love into our heart (Rom. 5:5). He empowers us to get on with the unifying, sanctifying, loving work of God. One's daily talk must be filled with praise and thanksgiving. A committed believer is so filled with the love of God that he frequently breaks out in song. In his singing he shares the goodness and powerful action of God (5:19). As one contemplates the blueprints of God and his own participation he is continually thankful. "Always giving thanks to God the Father for everything, in the name of our Lord Jesus Christ" (5:20).

Clearly the death of the Son, the life which he gave on our behalf, informs us day in and day out of the manner in which we are called to live. It is time to put aside lethargy, sluggishness, indecision. It is time to take up loving, giving up, sacrificing, submitting. We need to put our life where our commitment is. "Wake up, o sleeper, rise from the dead, and Christ will shine on you" (5:14).

Questions—Chapter 6

1. What is the basis for rules in Paul's letters?
2. What action of Christ underlies the rules in Ephesians 4 and 5?
3. How does the action of Christ define what Christians should not do?
4. In what specific ways is the cross to influence the life of believers?
5. What is the significance of the church in Ephesians?

Chapter 7

THE CROSS IN THE HOME AND IN BUSINESS (Ephesians 5:21-6:9)

At the end of chapter 4 and the beginning of chapter 5 Paul set the stage for what he plans to say about the way the Christian approaches his marriage, family, and occupation. The starting place is the love, death, sacrifice, and forgiveness of Christ (4:32-5:2). Paul has rules for marriage and so on. The rules are not spelled out in detail. Paul's approach is to set out the action of God which serves as the starting point, give a few clues as to how imitating God may be translated into human action, and then leave the details to be worked out by the believer. By pursuing this method Paul makes it clear that Christianity is not a rote memorization of and a rigorous adherence to a set of rules. It is rather the emulation of a model, the imitation of the life of Jesus Christ worked out and "fine tuned" according to one's situation. But Paul does not leave the believer floundering in a sea of uncertainty. He points to the heart of what Jesus revealed about God, and suggests initial lines of application. Christian morals and ethics therefore involve more than identifying, interpreting, and being certain about the nuances of the rules. We do not have, for example, a catalogue of 135 positive, and 173 negative rules in the New Testament. Rather we have a focusing in on the life of the Lord, an affirmation from those who knew him best as to what was central for his life and ministry, then a thinking through and working out how that can be replicated in the life of the believer.

Submit to One Another

If we accept the model of Christ then the key is submission. In his death he submitted to the will of the Father. Likewise he submitted his very life to those who believe for he "gave himself up for us as a fragrant offering" (5:2). The key principle therefore to be worked out in the marriage, the family, and one's occupation is, "Submit to one another out of reverence for Christ" (5:21). What does Paul mean, "out of reverence for Christ?" We revere someone by acting as they do. As the old saying goes the highest form of flattery is imitation. To revere Christ is to do as he does. What is it he does? He loves, gives, dies, forgives, sacrifices for others. When these traits characterize our lives we show reverence for Christ.

Wives and Husbands

First, we need to put marriage in perspective in Paul's vision. God's work in the universe is to unify it. We have made that point now too many times. The aspect of this unification in which man is involved is the church. The first priority in the life of the believer is the church. "We will in all things grow up into him who is the Head, that is, Christ" (4:15). Whether one is married or not—Paul wasn't—the Christian call involves the believer from morning until night in God's awesome work as a member of Christ's body. All of life contributes to this task—marriage, family, occupation. None of these are ends in themselves. They take their meaning rather from the contribution they make to the prior work of God.

Marriage has come in for difficult times. The root of the problem is secularization. For the secular person marriage is not related to anything in particular. It exists for its own ends. Those ends mostly involve self fulfillment and gratification. When these are called into question, when one partner can say, there's no longer anything in it for me, the marriage is finished. Unfortunately this attitude has spilled over into the church, because in fact secularization has spilled over into the church. Secularization in the church would not catch Paul by surprise. He saw it in these western Asia Minor churches. He just called it by a different name. "You must no longer live as the Gentiles do, in the futility of their thinking" (4:17). Paul might, however, be caught by surprise through the manner in which churches these days combat the erosion of marriage. Rather than sharing the Christian message that marriage is not an end in itself, churches and programs occasionally seem to contribute to the secular vision. For example, when a Christian messenger says one can get his life right by getting his marriage right he is making marriage an end in itself. That is laying more freight on marriage from a Christian perspective than it is able to bear. In fact, this false perspective on marriage may be contributing to marriage failures among Christians. In Paul's view what one must get right first is his relationship with God and an understanding that God has cut out as his life's goal the reconciling of humankind in the church. Whatever therefore marriage is relates to and correlates with that prior goal.

Marriage does in fact make an invaluable contribution to God's stellar plan. When a marriage tries to reflect the prior ways of Christ, the result is love, forgiveness, giving, sacrifice. Christian marriage takes its vision from the model of its Lord. "Submit to one another out of reverence for Christ" (5:21). Notice that the submitting is on both sides. Both the husband and the wife are to submit to each other. Some Christian proclaimers emphasize the submission on the part of the wife. Paul says that both are to submit. They are to submit to each other.

"Wives, submit to your husbands as to the Lord." Notice that wives are to submit, not because it is a rule of nature that man is the take charge person in the marriage, but "as to the Lord." The reason for the submission is that the Lord himself submitted to death on behalf of humankind. A further reason for the submission of the wife is that "the husband is the head of the wife as Christ is the head of the church" (5:23). But, in fact, this is the same reason. The church submits to Christ because he submitted first to it. "Christ loved us and gave himself up for us as a fragrant offering and sacrifice to God" (5:2). The church is the body of Christ. He gives the body direction but it is loving, tender, caring direction. After all the church is his own body. The headship of Christ is foreign to an authoritarian, harsh, "This is the way I see it, learn to like it" attitude. The phrase "his body, of which he is the Savior" (5:23) reiterates that the church submits to Christ because he has previously submitted to it. In like manner the wife accepts the headship of the husband because he has already become subject to her needs. He no more makes arbitrary demands on her than Christ makes on the church. The direction he gives is premised on his desire to serve his wife. "For even the Son of Man did not come to be served, but to serve, and to give his life as a ransom for many" (Mk. 10:45).

The points already made are borne out in the eloquent passage which follows. The husband is charged to love the wife just as Christ loved the church (5:25). Notice he *loved* and *gave*. My conclusion could be wrong, but as I see it, to love and serve are the same as to submit. So the charge to the husband is the same as to the wife, submit, love, give. In this manner the prior charge "Submit to one another," is spelled out. The point is not as some preach, namely, a distinction between submitting and loving. They are the same in regard to Christ. They are identical in regard to the husband and wife. The husband is, of course, charged with providing leadership in the marriage, but it is submitting leadership. It is a leadership in which the needs of the wife, when compatible with the ways of the Lord, are of first concern. The wife responds in kind to this leadership recognizing that it is loving and directed to her needs and concerns. Again pursuing the analogy between Christ and the church, Paul reiterates the love which motivates the decisions of the husband in relationship to his wife (5:28).

Paul has this peculiar idea, at least peculiar in our decade, that one realizes his desires and needs through looking after the other rather than looking after number one. The thesis in our time is that if we don't look out for number one no one will. Paul thinks we are realized, our needs are met, not through demands, but mutuality. In a healthy relationship, if we respond to the needs of the other, they in turn are inclined to respond to our needs. That relationship is carried through in a much better spirit and is more fulfilling than a relationship based on demands. We have travelled with couples under various arrangements. Perhaps the most congenial involved a week's trip to Denver to a convention. At the first meal the other couple said why don't we pay for this meal and you get the next one. That worked well. We never had to worry about how to divide up the check after each meal. The same approach works well in marriage. Submit to the other. Look out as to how the mate's lot can be improved. You will be surprised how in turn he or she seeks to improve your lot. Of course, there are sick people and Paul certainly wouldn't recommend an approach of this sort in such cases. Sick people enjoy either punishing or being punished as the case may be. Paul knew such people. He called them sinners. "Having lost all sensitivity, they have given themselves over to sensuality so as to indulge in every kind of impurity, with a continual lust for more" (4:19).

A good, Christ-based marriage contributes immeasurably to the unifying of mankind in the church. Paul recognizes this in 5:22-23 for he moves readily from the love which flows between husband and wife and that between Christ and the church. He is also interested in the love that moves back to Christ as head. In the mystery about a man leaving his father and mother (5:31-32) the point seems to be that, just as in marriage where husband and wife leave other relations to be united, so those in the church leave other relationships to be singularly united with Christ. The one who learns to love through marriage has gained much valuable experience so as to better exercise love in the church and hence contribute to God's plan to unify mankind through the church. I can myself attest to the fact that most of what I have learned about real love has been through marriage. It's not that my wife was so much superior at loving than I. Rather, we together have learned the contours of deep and profound Christian love. It has taken thirty years and we are still learning.

Of course, one doesn't need marriage to learn what we did. Paul didn't. But one does need people. Paul was people oriented. He was other oriented because in his view Christ called him to it. I see a problem in the movement toward single living in our time. I think Christian messengers need to be careful how they speak about and relate to singles. It is true that for Paul the state of marriage has no priority over the single state (1 Cor. 7:8). The church obviously is to welcome and to incorporate singles into the body. But the church needs to speak plainly to the fact that the singles just like Paul, are called to devote their life to service and the cultivating of loving relationships with others. Much single living these days is premised on the thesis, "I want to live my life my own way." This philosophy of single living is self serving. The church must take care in its single's ministry not to contribute to the "Me Generation" self-centeredness. In the plan of God the call is larger than any individual. It is a call to join hands with God in the church to reconcile all men to himself.

Children and Parents

The principles that obtain in the case of the wife and husband also apply to children and parents. "Children, obey your parents in the Lord" (6:1). Christ obeyed or submitted. It is therefore Christlike to submit to parents. The phrase "in the Lord" is a correct translation. As it stands it may mean only insofar as the orders of the parents comply with the ways of the Lord. Surely Paul does not mean that a child need not obey a parent who is not a Christian. The fact is he is writing to Christian families. The best way to take the phrase is to see it as 5:22 "as to the Lord." In other words the reason children in Christian families need to submit to their parents is that Christ submitted. For Christians Paul proposes actions commensurate with their commitment to Christ. God holds them responsible to Christ because they have committed their life to him. He holds those outside Christ responsible, but not because of Christ (1 Cor. 5:13). Christian ethics are not universal ethics. They are ethics which take their beginning point from the life and death of Christ.

I would suggest further that the phrase, "Submit to one another" (5:21) applies to the parent-child relationship. While Paul does not explicitly say so, he does charge the fathers, "do not exasperate your children" (6:4). Submitting to the children, as with the wife, does not mean complying with every whim and want. It means with the love and giving of the Lord in mind to arrange for their best interests. As with the spouse, so healthy children respond in kind if the approach is genuine love and care. They are to be brought up "in the training and instruction of the Lord" (6:4). That means loving as he loved, and giving as he gave.

Slaves and Masters

The response of the slave to the master likewise keeps an eye on the Christ who served (6:5). In this case the master may not be a Christian and it is indeed possible that he won't respond in kind. The Christian slave will behave as a hard working slave regardless. He knows that he will be rewarded by Christ his master even if not by his earthly master (6:8). So slaves are to submit to their masters out of reverence for Christ. Christian masters likewise are to submit to their slaves. That does not mean, as we have seen, to take orders from the slaves, but to act in such a manner that it is in the best interests of the slaves. To do so is to recognize Christ as master. He lived in the best interest of others, not just his own. An employer who makes plans which are in the best interests of the employees can expect like treatment from his employees.

My greatgrandfather, John Taylor, grew up in northern Alabama. Prior to the Civil War he was a slave overseer on a plantation near Florence. He was not an avid defender of slavery, but that was his upbringing. He believed that slaves will treat their masters as he treats them. He therefore fed and cared for the slaves under his charge as best as permitted. His conviction was that as the result he got much more work out of his slaves than did most overseers. "Submit to one another out of reverence for Christ" (5:21). If an employer today has the best interests of his employees at heart, they will have his best interests at heart.

In every situation, in all the aspects of life, the Christian is working to make giving, love, sharing, and unity the prime reality. In that manner he is doing his best to contribute to the eventuation of the great dream of God, "to bring all things in heaven and on earth together under one head, even Christ" (Eph. 1:10).

Questions—Chapter 7

1. Why are Christians to submit?
2. What are the implications of submitting in marriage?
3. What are the implications of submitting in the family?
4. What are the implications of submitting in one's work?
5. Is there a problem with the current popularity of single living?

Chapter 8

THE BATTLE FOR THE UNIVERSE (Ephesians 6:10-24)

The plan God put on the drawing boards "before the creation of the world" (1:4) was of cosmic magnitude. The astounding news is that the battle in which God has enlisted Christians is a cosmic battle. We are accustomed these days in movies and on television to find ourselves in the midst of an interplanetary, or intergalactic war. The Star Wars saga defies the imagination in respect to how far reaching future wars may become. None of these current visions, however, compare with that of Paul. The battle in which the Christian is engaged has to do, not with some region of the universe, but with the universe itself. Furthermore, it extends beyond human types, however diverse, as in science fiction. The battle for the universe involves a distinct species of beings who are not flesh and blood (6:12).

Our Christian calling thereupon is a heady one indeed! Our action from day to day is more than meets the eye. If life needs a super purpose to give it spice and meaning, surely the blueprint for the Christian life as outlined by Paul in Ephesians measures up on all counts. If anyone ever needed a reason for getting up in the morning, this is it! The Christian battle encompasses all that is in the universe, whether visible to the human eye or not. We can react to this battle in two ways. One is in excitement, the adrenalin flowing freely, in anticipation that since God goes along with the believer the outcome is assured. The response, however, could be the opposite. We could conclude that since we are in a death grip struggle with awesome, evil, superhuman powers, we can't say we are really up to all that and want no part of it.

Man does not have the option in Paul's thinking as to whether to enlist or not. In the battle for the universe there is no demilitarized zone. The battle rages fierce in every cosmic region. No one can declare a non-combatant status. There is no such thing as neutrality. Whether one desires it, sooner or later he is going to get caught in the cross fire. For Paul there are only two sorts of humans—those who follow the ways of this world and the ruler of the kingdom of the air (2:2), and those alive with Christ seated with him in the heavenly regions (2:5-6). If one has not enlisted in the army of the Lord he automatically is conscripted by the "powers of this dark world" (6:12).

The battle plan of God in which the Christian is engaged is awesome and mind boggling. While one moment we may feel greatly affirmed that we have been asked to serve on God's team, the next moment we may be overcome with fear because of the dangers that lurk on every side. With just cause we may consider the opposing forces more than we can face up to. We may feel compelled to look around every corner, behind every tree, and under every stone before we make a single move. Paul wants to make it perfectly clear that while the battle is real, we are not without recourse. The God who enlisted us is head of the number one empire in the universe. He will see to it that we are equipped for the fight. All we need to do is utilize the equipment he provides.

The Battle Rages

It is obvious that for Paul the victory of Christ was the turning point of history. "And God placed all things under his feet and appointed him to be head over everything for the church, which is his body, the fullness of him who fills everything in every way" (1:22-23). So great was the victory of Christ in the death and resurrection that the believer as the result is "raised . . . up with Christ and seated . . . with him in the heavenly realms in Christ Jesus" (Eph. 2:6). In the life and death of Christ a strategic skirmish was won. A beachhead was established which will never again revert to the enemy. Though Paul thought a great battle was won in the death and resurrection, he was not of the opinion that the war was over. Even though the believer is now seated in the heavenly realms in Christ Jesus, that is not the end. He still awaits the future "in order that in the coming ages he might show the incomparable riches of his grace." At that time the battle for the universe will be over. Because of the beachhead already established, it is obvious who will win. At that time the plan of God to reconcile everything to himself through the Son, Jesus Christ, in the church will be realized. At present, however, the battle is fierce and real. "For our struggle is not against flesh and blood" (Eph. 6:12).

In Ephesians the battle of God for the universe seems more on the way toward fruition than, for example, in Romans. There Paul seems to characterize the present as one of defeat and suffering and not as triumphal as Ephesians 6:2. "I consider that our present sufferings are not worth comparing with the glory that will be revealed in us" (Rom. 8:18). Even in Romans, however, Paul was clear about the achievement of Christ. Already he has won the victory over sin, death, and the law. But it is the case that Paul speaks more plainly of the realized work of God in Ephesians. Critical scholars cite the movement toward "realized eschatology" as a factor in their denying Pauline authorship of Ephesians.

Two reasons are immediately forthcoming as to why in Ephesians Paul exhibits a movement toward realized eschatology. (This terminology simply means that in the earthly appearance of Christ he realized all that is to be realized. "Eschatology" in Greek has to do with end things.) First, Paul upon his arrival in Rome concluded that God's work was farther down the road. He saw his proclamation of the Gospel in Rome another major stage in the completion of God's plan. For that reason Ephesians should represent a more triumphal spirit than Paul's earlier letters. But second, and perhaps more important, some in Asia Minor argued that in his earthly appearance the Christ fully completed the task to which God assigned him. For the one who received in faith the work of the Christ, history already was at an end. The believer in the know is already living beyond time and history. He is already caught up into the heavenly regions. Several passages in the New Testament allude to this point of view which we may label "overly realized eschatology." The clearest instance is in 2 Timothy. Paul there speaks of a point of view which has secured various adherents. He names two. "Avoid godless chatter, because those who indulge in it will become more and more ungodly. Their teaching will spread like gangrene.

Among them are Hymenaeus and Philetus, who have wandered away from the truth. They say that the resurrection has already taken place, and they destroy the faith of some" (2 Tim. 2:16-18). Paul, therefore, in effect agreed in Ephesians that what Christ accomplished places humans in a new situation in history. He did not, however, concur that it lifts them beyond history.

Some Christians known by Paul had moved toward realized eschatology. The most advanced were already there. Though one finds movement toward realized eschatology in Paul's later writings, his view is consistently the same and can be described as "inaugurated" eschatology. Through his death and resurrection Jesus won a great battle. The end of the war is assured. But numerous skirmishes are still to be fought. An excellent illustration comes from World War II and is especially meaningful to those of us who spent many a night glued to the radio hoping for good news. The crucial battle on the European front was the invasion of Normandy Beach on the French coast. The code name for that invasion was D-Day. D-Day was not V-Day, that is the end of the war. But as we sat by the radio and heard the unbelievable story of the beachhead established at Normandy we knew that the war would never be the same again. Already we were in the driver's seat. We were well aware that months of mop-up operations lay ahead. Because of D-Day, however, V-Day was assured. Likewise with Paul. The resurrection of Christ assured the ultimate resurrection of all believers and reconciliation of the universe to God. The first major skirmish was won. Paul did not see how anyone could look at the war in the same manner again. The believer, however, still lives in history, fighting battles from day to day, but ever in confidence that the battle for the universe will ultimately announce God as the winner.

Put on the Full Armor

The watchful, alert Christian enters the fray properly equipped and prepared, anxious for combat. The believer has no reason for fear. "Finally, be strong in the Lord in his mighty power" (6:10). He knows God will emerge as the eventual winner. He knows that God will go with him and protect him if he employs the issued equipment. Not every day is the same in battle. Some days the enemy will hardly be visible. But one must always be ready for the attack. "Therefore put on the full armor of God, so that when the day of evil comes, you may be able to stand your ground" (6:13). The equipment needed all comes from God: truth, righteousness, gospel of peace, faith, salvation, the Spirit. God provides or makes possible all this equipment. We must, however, reach forth and receive the kingdom's equipment. Then once issued, we must put it on or carry it into battle. These battle pieces relate to the unity in God which some day he is going to bring to full realization. One of the main strategies in battle is prayer. God responds to prayer. It makes all the difference in the world. It puts us in the mood to let God act powerfully on our behalf. "And pray in the Spirit on all occasions with all kinds of prayers and requests" (6:18). What does Paul mean, "pray in the Spirit?" Actually from the Greek, since the article is missing, it is not certain that the Holy Spirit is intended. Is this some special prayer-type? That seems unlikely since praying in the Spirit involves all kinds of prayers (6:18). I take it he has in mind prayer in which one is completely open to the Spirit, so He may assist the believer in praying for what is God's will (Rom. 8:26-27).

As he closes the letter, Paul asks for prayer on his own behalf so that he may declare the right words as he ministers from his Roman imprisonment (6:19-20). There are many other things Paul would like to tell them. As we indicated in the first chapter Paul always felt a deep personal responsibility for those he brought to Christ, and for their converts. To show his personal interest and consideration Paul has asked Tychicus to share with them personal information, and the results of his ministry. In view of the great message of the epistle our appreciation for the concluding words "peace," "love," and "grace" is greatly enhanced. So powerful are the actions of God behind these words that they elicit an "undying love" from the believer (6:24).

Conclusion

How can one offer concluding remarks about Ephesians? The more one works on the message, the more astonished and over-awed one becomes. One simply has to say I wasn't fully aware of all the ramifications of the death and resurrection of Jesus Christ. I wasn't fully cognizant of the unprecedented work of reconciliation in which I am here and now involved. I haven't been fully attuned to the implications of the love and death of Christ for all the facets of life. At this point all I can do is cry out in humble praise and adoration. I can only with greater determination plunge into the incomparable work of the kingdom. I can now fully identify with Paul in closing the doctrinal section of the letter. "Now to him who is able to do immeasurably more than all we ask or imagine, according to his power that is at work within us, to him be glory in the church and in Christ Jesus throughout all generations, for ever and ever! Amen" (3:20-21).

Questions—Chapter 8

1. How does the battle for the universe shape up in Ephesians?
2. Who are the "spiritual forces" of evil?
3. How does Paul regard the death of Christ in respect to this battle? Comment on "inaugurated" eschatology.
4. How should Christians react to this battle?
5. How can they be properly equipped?

Chapter 9

COLOSSIANS: THE REGION, THE CHURCH, THE MESSAGE

Since the Colossian letter is to a specific church and since it has affinities with Philemon we know more about its recipients and the local situation than we do with Ephesians. As with Ephesians this is an impressive and awesome presentation of the role of Christ in the universe. Ephesians stresses the unity which Christ brings to the cosmos through his work and that of the Holy Spirit in the church. Colossians centers in on who Christ is, as compared with other heavenly beings, and what he accomplished in his death. As with Ephesians, the practical implications of the theology are spelled out in the latter half of the Epistle. From these observations we conclude that here Paul is chiefly concerned with the erosion of the role of Christ, while in Ephesians he is anxious over the unity of the churches and the manner in which God, Christ, and the Holy Spirit effect this unity. This difference is in part explained if Colossians is a letter to one church and Ephesians a letter to be circulated among many churches.

The Region

If one turns to a map of Paul's mission journeys, he locates Colossae in the Roman Province of Asia. In the twentieth century it is located in southwestern Turkey. Two other cities with Colossae formed a triangle. About twelve miles to the west lay Laodicea and twelve miles to the north, Hierapolis. Colossae was the principal city in 401 B.C. according to Xenophon, who passed through with the retreating army of Cyrus. By Paul's time Colossae was overshadowed by Hierapolis and Laodicea, both mentioned in the epistle (4:13).

According to Strabo its main commercial product was fine black wool. The nearest major port city was Ephesus, eighty miles northwest. It was therefore tied culturally and commercially to that hub city. Toward the end of the first century Colossae was destroyed by an earthquake and never rebuilt. In the nineteenth century a theatre and acropolis were discovered through excavation, but little else. The population in the first century consisted of indigenous Phrygian and Greek settlers and several Jewish colonists who had moved in during the reign of Antiochus the Great (223-187 B.C.).

The Church

The Roman province of Asia was evangelized by converts of Paul who visited the surrounding towns while he planted the church on a solid basis in Ephesus from 53 to 56 A.D. Paul never visited Colossae prior to this letter, "We have heard of your faith in Christ Jesus" (1:4). "For this reason, since the day we heard about you, we have not stopped praying for you" (1:9). But he considered the church within his pastoral concerns because it was planted by Epaphras, a convert of his, probably during his Ephesian ministry. Epaphras was a native of Colossae (4:12) and no doubt was so impressed with his newly found faith that with Paul's encouragement he decided to return home and share it with his relatives, friends and neighbors. His efforts obviously met with considerable success. We know something of the advance of Christianity in the region through the alarm of Demetrius the Ephesian silversmith whose livelihood involved the production of replicas of the goddess Artemis. In addressing his fellow craftsmen he remarked, "And you see and hear how this fellow Paul has convinced and led astray large numbers of people here in Ephesus and in practically the whole province of Asia" (Acts 19:26). Demetrius obviously was guilty of rhetorical exaggeration, but his claim was not without substance as we know from the churches in the region named in the New Testament.

We can say a few words about the churches in the region. Philemon, to whom the epistle by the same name was addressed, probably lived in Colossae. We read that a church met in his house (Philemon 2). In Colossians 4:15 we read about a certain Nympha and the church which met in her house. A dispute exists at two points. My view is that Nympha was a woman who likely lived in Colossae, though Laodicea cannot be ruled out. If this supposition is correct we know of a least two house churches in Colossae. The early Christians met in houses of the more affluent members. As the disciples multiplied and the first place of meeting became crowded they either moved to a larger domicile or an additional house. Even with multiple meeting places churches in a locality were addressed as a single church and probably were under the oversight of one eldership. By looking at the grouping of the names in Romans 16 it appears that at least three house churches existed in Rome when Paul wrote the letter to that city. His letter in that case was addressed "To all in Rome who are loved by God and called to be saints" (1:7). In Titus, Paul instructed this fellow worker to "appoint elders in every town" (1:5). In the tri-cities of Colossae, Hierapolis, and Laodicea we know that groups also met in Laodicea and Hierapolis (Col. 4:13). These churches apparently had close ties and were all founded by Epaphras (4:12,13). How many churches and Christians may have been in the tri-cities is difficult to estimate. We can suppose 40 to 60 persons meeting in a house church. Whether there were more than one house church in the other towns in unknown, but in view of their larger size it is not unlikely.

Despite the fact that Paul had never visited Colossae he knew persons from there and apparently through the years dispatched several fellow workers for visits. Colossians and Philemon both contain a list of persons (almost identical) who send greetings from Rome. Not all of these individuals had visited Colossae, but the Colossians knew enough about Paul and his fellow workers so that they were familiar with the names cited. Paul addressed persons in Colossae with endearing terms. Either he had met them on some occasion, possibly they visited him during his long stay in Ephesus, or else he had heard much about them. He wrote in Philemon (1,2) "To Philemon our dear friend and fellow worker, to Apphia our sister, to Archippus our fellow soldier and to the church. . . ." One might conclude that Paul was presumptive in the manner in which he wrote Philemon unless he personally knew the man. But then Paul spoke straight from the shoulder when in his opinion the situation demanded.

In Rome Paul heard rumblings from Colossae. Before long

he dispatched a letter with a man by the name of Tychicus. Tychicus is called an Asian (Acts 20:4) perhaps from Ephesus,(2 Tim. 4:12), at least not from Colossae since Paul includes an introduction. "He is a dear brother, a faithful minister and fellow servant in the Lord" (Col. 4:7). Traveling with Tychicus was a runaway slave by the name of Onesimus whom Paul converted and persuaded to return to Philemon his master (Col. 4:9, Philemon 8-16). Tychicus carried several letters from Paul: Colossians, the letter to Philemon, one to the church at Laodicea (Col. 4:16), and likely Ephesians. Some have proposed that the letter to the Laodiceans is in fact Ephesians since that letter was originally undesignated. Such seems quite unlikely, however, in view of the lack of the personal references of the sort found in Colossians. Paul probably was informed of the divergent views in the church at Colossae by Epaphras (Col. 4:12). It could be that the letter was in part written to hold up the hands of Archippus. "See to it that you complete the work you have received in the Lord" (4:17). Or contrariwise that Archippus was a reluctant opponent to these wayward views and this note is a charge for him to take a firmer stand.

What were the views which concerned Paul? From reading the letter, partly between the lines, we surmise the following: 1). They had a story of a heavenly messenger who revealed the mystery (1:26, 2:2) whereby those believing were granted entry into the kingdom of light (1:12). 2). Their elaboration on that mystery was referred to by Paul as a "hollow and deceptive philosophy" (2:8). 3). Their mystery involved heavenly beings referred to as "stoicheion"—best translated with the RSV "elemental spirits of the universe" (2:8, 2:20). Included within this category are "rulers, powers, and authorities" (1:16, 2:9, 2:15), and angels (2:18). (The NIV translation of "stoicheion," "the basic principles of this world" in my opinion is not helpful as I will argue later.) These beings were worshiped. Christ was not ignored. He was simply added to the rest as one heavenly power among many. (2:9,10). 4). Showing proper deference to the "stoicheion" involved strict observation of a number of rules, mostly having to do with abstinence and self denial (2:20-23). 5). Jewish elements also commended themselves, including circumcision (2:11), food regulations (2:16), religious festivals, new moons, and sabbaths (2:16). 6). Spiritual visions were claimed (2:18). 7) Loose morals may have been involved

(3:5-10). 8). A degree of superiority may have been assigned to those of Jewish background (3:11).

It becomes immediately obvious that the spurious views Paul confronted at Colossae possess many of the features behind the Ephesians letter, which in chapter 2 we labeled as "incipient Gnosticism." The main difference is specificity, such as references to angels, rules for self denial, specific Jewish customs, and visions. All these are found in second century Gnostic systems. From what we have learned from the problems addressed by Paul in these two letters, I conclude that some Jews from a sycretistic background with heavenly myths and visions, were converted to the faith. Christianity appealed to them because it included a story of divine action by a heavenly figure, that is Jesus Christ, and was not scrupulous in keeping all the Jewish regulations. Jesus was added to their panoply of heavenly beings, but was not assigned a superior role. These Jews, after entering the church, continued to elaborate on their myths (1 Tim. 1:4) and interested certain members with their fantastic stories. Most of the Colossian Christians, however, were from a Gentile background. As we have already noticed in Ephesians, taking up these mythical outlooks undercut a number of the fundamentals of the Christian faith.

The Message

Paul's approach was not simply negation. He knew well the battle for minds is not won by denying everything another affirms. Rather, at several points he took over their vocabulary and conceptions, then indicated how Christianity has the true or superior version. His response to the heavenly mystery in which one is inducted into a kingdom of light, was that the true mystery has to do with what Christ accomplished through his death on earth (1:20). It has nothing to do with a concocted heavenly drama. Those who receive Christ as Lord are in fact inducted into the kingdom of light (1:12).

Foremost, Paul challenged the view that in terms of heavenly beings, Christ is just one among many. For Paul, Christ is not just a run-of-the-mill angelic figure. Rather, "In Christ all the fullness of the Deity lives in bodily form" (2:9). Because of who he is, he is not one of many powers, but "is the head over every power and authority" (2:10). "He is the image of the invisible God, the firstborn over all creation. For by him all things were created: things in heaven and on earth, visible and invisible. . . . He is before all things, and in him all things hold together" (1:15-17). Whatever these other powers may be, however dear to certain ones in the Colossian church, they are of little consequence when compared with Christ. For that reason homage to these beings is ridiculous. "And you have been given fullness in Christ" (2:10). There is simply no ground for showing deference to heavenly beings, angels, or self-denying rules claimed in their name.

Because of the victory of Christ for the church he is the one Christians adore. The believer should not be distracted or starry-eyed over rival claims. "Once you were alienated from God and were enemies in your minds because of your evil behavior. But now he has reconciled you by Christ's physical body through death to present you holy in his sight, without blemish and free from accusation" (1:21,22). Christ through his death put aside special powers claimed for Jewish rites (2:11-17), for angels and unusual visions (2:18), for moral license (3:5-10), and for Jewishness (3:11).

The heart of Paul's message to the Colossians lies in 1:13, "For he has rescued us from the dominion of darkness and brought us into the kingdom of the Son he loves, in whom we have redemption, the forgiveness of sins."

Questions—Chapter 9

1. How does knowing about the region help understand Colossians?
2. How was the church started at Colossae?
3. Why did Paul write to the Colossians?
4. What were the views to which he responded?
5. What was Paul's basic way of responding?

Chapter 10

CHRIST: WHO HE IS AND WHAT HE ACCOMPLISHED (Colossians 1:1-23)

Paul has a great respect for the Christian believers at Colossae as he does for believers everywhere. "To the holy and faithful brothers in Christ at Colossae" (1:2). He writes of his thanks to God for their "faith in Christ Jesus and the love you have for all the saints" (1:4). He mentions his warm regards for Epaphras "our dear fellow servant, who is a faithful minister of Christ on our behalf" (1:7). It was this close brother who told Paul of their "love in the spirit" (1:8). (Interestingly, this is the only instance in which Paul speaks of the Holy Spirit in Colossians, possibly thereby to highlight the significance of Christ.) He also writes in glowing terms of the success of the gospel. Reflecting on the accumulated growth while imprisoned in Rome especially reassured Paul, resulting in expansive prose, and confidence in God's untimate winning over of humankind. "All over the world this gospel is producing fruit and growing" (1:6).

Paul therefore expresses concern for the Colossian Christians and prays they will exhibit the full implications of the gospel. That was Paul's hope for all believers. He writes in expectation that his remarks, coupled with their searching, will enable them to "live a life worthy of the Lord and may please him in every way: bearing fruit in every good work, growing in the knowledge of God" (1:10). Paul's comments throughout chapter 1 are instructive. He is aware of certain forces, perhaps mostly exterior, making inroads inimical to the Christian faith. But he does not presume to disfellowship anyone. Apparently he is of the conviction that by setting forth the genuine message in the thought patterns and vocabulary of these local religionists he will change their understanding and win them over.

Paul's expectations differ from ours. In our religious climate two attitudes are prevalent. One is that everyone has a right to his own opinion or interpretation therefore no effort should be made to win over those differing. The other holds that when people start paying attention to unsound positions we cannot hope to win them over. The only thing to do is to ask them to move on. If they don't think our way we must either put them down or out. Paul shared neither of these convictions. He affirmed that there are correct understandings of the Christian faith and false ones. He believed that when false concepts show up you deal with them head on by pleading, denouncing, and imploring. He believed you keep people around rather than forcing them out, precisely so you may have a chance to bring them around. If you are no longer in communication that chance disappears.

The Central Message

In chapter nine we suggested that 1:13 is the center of the message to the Colossians. In this statement Paul announces the unparalleled news which is bed rock for the Christian faith. "For he has rescued us from the dominion of darkness and brought us into the kingdom of the Son he loves, in whom we have redemption, the forgiveness of sins." Those in Asia Minor with contorted legends claim that entry into the kingdom of light results from recounting a heavenly drama involving a hierarchy of beings in different spheres of the cosmos. This dramatic account is not public information. It is an inside mystery and only obtainable from those in the know (1:13). Paul does not contest a drama of salvation, and there is indeed a kingdom of light. It is in fact the case that people inhabit the kingdom of darkness until they accept God's offer for entry into the kingdom of light.

The real story is that it is God himself who has rescued us from darkness. Salvation is not through a set of esoteric angelic beings. Neither is it through a specially gifted human religious leader, nor strict adherence to a set of divine or human rules. It is God himself, who out of unrelenting love made special and far reaching arrangements for our transference from darkness into light. Even in today's times we have persons with special stories and offers of salvation. Salvation is not a human commodity dispensable through a divine franchise. God himself arranged it, and he retains for himself all the rights of distribution. The means through which God dispenses salvation is "the Son he loves."

Paul doesn't deny the reality of heavenly beings, powers, angels and so on. These beings, however, simply are not the channel through which God snatched man from the kingdom of darkness. "Redemption, the forgiveness of sins" is through one being—the Son God loves. He is distinguished from every other power whether in heaven or on earth. The real divine drama took place, not in the cosmos, but on earth and in the divine Son who took on the flesh of men (1:22). The passage way to the kingdom is not a guarded mystery, nor a pipeline to some invisible region. Rather the cosmic event occured right on earth where it was witnessed by humankind. "For God so loved the world that he gave his only Son." So much did he love the world that his spectacular act of reconciliation took place on earth.

Colossians 1:13 gets to the heart of the epistle. Amplification in the remainder declares who the beloved Son is, and what he accomplished in his death and resurrection. From there Paul shows that whatever other powers exist, their significance evaporates when compared with that of the Son God loves. In the last two chapters he sets out the ramifications of the action of Christ for the day to day routine of Christian life. "Since, then, you have been raised with Christ, set your hearts on things above, where Christ is seated at the right hand of God" (3:1).

All God's Fullness Dwells in Him

Because of who Christ is and what he accomplished through his death he stands head and shoulders above any powers whatever in the universe. First, the Son is the image of God. This means that just as the reflection in the mirror is the exact reproduction of a person, so Christ is the exact reproduction of God. In the Old Testament a child is said to be the image of the father, so Seth of Adam (Gen. 5:3). If there is any revealer of God, any penetration of the mystery, it is Jesus, Son of God, not some heavenly messenger from a sphere of the cosmos. God is invisible. Jesus as the image of God, by making an appearance on earth, became visible. Furthermore, he is the "firstborn" of all creation. He is superior to any of the heavenly beings because he is prior to them all. In fact, he was the agent through whom God made everything that was made whether in heaven or on earth. Of foremost significance, considering the views of those addressed, is the fact that through him were created things visible and invisible "whether thrones or powers or rulers or authorities" (1:16).

Notice that Paul does not deny the existence of powers in heavenly regions. In fact, in Ephesians Paul contended that certain of these powers are evil (Eph. 6:12). So if anyone at Colossae cited a specific heavenly being as his source of inside information, or as especially worthy of adoration, Paul did not attempt to deny his existence. He simply contended that people who pay attention to such powers must be out of their mind, since the one who created them all elicits their following. Even today beings unseen by us may play far more significant roles than we imagine. Occasionally, someone makes the discovery, new to them, of the power and significance of angels or angelic beings. While all of this is exciting and may in fact have some substance, one has to question the importance of their find, if all along they have been obedient to Christ and known his power.

Even in America these days inordinate attention is paid to suprasensible powers, and channels through which these resources may be tapped. Paul's response would be, why all the effort, money, and time when there is available power from the one who stands head and shoulders above them all? A word might also be said in respect to mission efforts in regions of the world where primitive religions persist. These peoples have their gods, their invisible beings and forces. It is a long range, perhaps thankless task to convince these people that such forces are figments of their imagination. Apparently Paul would not work at it from that end. Rather, he would announce who Christ is. He is the power who stands above all others. If one wishes to tap power at the source, look to Christ. One needs show obeisance to, and worry about one power only.

When Christ is taken seriously as the supreme power in the universe then the other powers recede farther and farther toward the horizon and eventually disappear. The highways of history are strewn with heavenly beings who once had a death grip on peoples, but now are known only to historians and tourists.

A word needs to be said about the section before us, 1:15-20. Scholars these days believe that this section is hymnic in form. The evidence is solidly founded. The question is, what is the source of the hymn? Is Paul himself the author? Most scholars assume not, though they think he has added here and there so as to get his points in. If not Paul, who? Different schools of thought vie for aceptance, but none as yet has won a consensus. Most Bultmannians assume that this was a Gnostic hymn which Paul rewrote so as to change the theology. Others who don't believe Gnosticism was this early argue that it is a Hellensitic hymn taken over and Christianized. A few are open to Christian origins. The best proposal, in my thinking, is that Paul has revised an old pre-Christian hymn from syncretized Judaism which incorporated wisdom motifs. I have already offered such backgrounds as the roots of incipient Gnosticism at Colossae. Borrowings of this sort continue even to this day. "Edelweiss" from *Sound of Music* has been supplied with Christian words, even retaining some of the lines from the original. My sister-in-law who with my brother spent nine years working with a German and an American congregation in Nuremberg has said on more than one occasion that she sings with reluctance certain popular American hymns because they are based on German drinking songs.

What are the clues that this hymn may have Jewish wisdom roots? By the first century, wisdom was personified to be God's divine helper in creation. A number of Old Testament and extra-Biblical passages may be cited as sources for projecting a creation helper. Here we cite parts of Proverbs 8, which in turn has as a backdrop Genesis 1 and various creation psalms. "The Lord possessed me at the beginning of his work, before his deeds of old; I was appointed from eternity, from the beginning, before the world began . . . I was there when he set the heavens in place, when he marked out the horizon on the face of the deep . . . Then I was the craftsman at his side. I was filled with delight day after day, rejoicing always in his presence (Prov. 8:22-31). One can readily see parallels between language and conception here and that in Colossians 1:15-20. Regardless, Paul takes it over and incorporates specific Christian affirmations. The hymn as revised is now a profound proclamation concerning the Son God loves.

By Christ's Physical Body

With verse 17 the work of Christ is set out. Since he is before all things and all things came through him he holds all things together. He is head especially of the church, and since he is supreme in the universe, its position is secured (1:18). Other deities and angelic beings may possess certain divine like qualities, more or less. He stands above them all because "God was pleased to have all his fullness dwell in him" (1:19). He came to the earth, shed his blood on the cross (1:20) and through his blood reconciled everything to God, whether on earth or in heaven. Because of who he is and what he did he is the one to whom the believer must show deference and homage. The Supreme act of God was on earth, not in heaven. It was human death with genuine human blood which rearranged heaven and earth.

Paul ends (1:21-23) with an exhortation for the believers to remain true to the Christian vision. They should shun pre-Christian actions. Formerly they were apart from God. Now because of Christ and his physical death they are "holy in his sight, without blemish and free from accusation" (1:22). They therefore must continue in and support Christ's action rather than its inferior rivals. Those who take up other salvation stories, however, new, exciting, and original, will find themselves out on the end of a limb. The only real hope for salvation is found in the gospel of Christ (1:23).

Paul calls the Colossians to this gospel because it has been universally announced. The stories they are toying with have mostly local circulation. We are caught somewhat off guard by Paul's declaration that the gospel has been "proclaimed to every creature under heaven" (1:23). What can Paul mean by that? Surely he did not believe that every last individual had heard. In the context I think foremost in his mind is the fact that the true Christian gospel is not something esoteric to be whispered behind closed doors or in secret inner sanctuaries.

The Christian mystery took place openly. Its announcements are public announcements to every creature under Heaven. In contrast with the secretive, confidential cosmic dramas of the syncretizers, the true Christian message opts to go public. It is a message for all men, not just a chosen few. The statement is obviously a hyperbole. But what else can it mean? For Paul an area was evangelized when a beachhead was established in a key communications center. Out of that center the gospel radiates to the towns, villages, and hamlets (Rom. 15:17-24). "So from Jerusalem all the way around to Illyricum, I have fully proclaimed the gospel of Christ" (Rom. 15:19). Rome itself was a key city inasmuch as it was the hub of the empire. Paul had in mind that public announcements had been made in the strategic cities and was in the process of radiating to "every creature under heaven."

Questions—Chapter 10

1. How does Paul handle persons with whom he disagrees?
2. What is the central message of Colossians?
3. What view of who Christ is does Paul offer in Colossians?
4. What are the implications of the death of Christ in Colossians 1?
5. What does Paul mean that the gospel has been preached to "every creature"?

Chapter 11

LIVING UNDER THE LORDSHIP OF CHRIST (Colossians 1:24-2:23)

Paul clearly declared the Lordship of Christ over the whole cosmos. "He is before all things, and in him all things hold together. And he is the head of the body, the church; he is the beginning and the firstborn from among the dead, so that in everything he might have the supremacy" (Col. 1:17,18). What are the ramifications of the Lordship of Christ for the believer on various fronts? In Colossians 1:24-2:23 Paul lays out the concrete implications as he sees them.

For the Sake of His Body

Just as the Lord of the church suffered to bring reconciliation to the universe, even now, the church which is his body, suffers. Suffering is the means through which a torn, diseased, dissipated world, is healed and reconciled. Healing can't take place in another realm. It takes place right here. Earth is the stage on which the salvific drama of God is played. The significance of the earth, the church, man, hence becomes obvious. We are overawed by the significance of the believer's role in the universe. We cannot imagine that we or our work can be all that important. In such a mood we cry out with the Psalmist, "What is man that you are mindful of him, the son of man that you care for him? You made him a little lower than the heavenly beings and crowned him with glory and honor" (8:4,5).

Paul rejoices that he is permitted to suffer as did his Lord. He may also have in mind that Jesus spoke of woes preceding the end, and the coming again of the Lord Jesus Christ (Mk.

13:7-13, 28-37). His rejoicing may also be that his imprisonment anticipates the end of history. He even conceives his suffering as the continuation of the work of Christ; as boosting it farther on the route to fruition. His suffering is not only because of Christ, but on behalf of the church. Paul's suffering serves as an example that the church hastens the coming of the Lord by its suffering. Paul rejected salvation by works, but in some measure believed in consummation by works. He believed that the proclamation, suffering and labor of Christians paved the way for the coming again of its Lord. Of course, he had no pat formula for how to force that day. It would be the Lord's day, and at his good pleasure. But human effort in the church for Paul made a difference. Very clearly then the first implication is that Lordship involves suffering. Suffering is a channel through which God brings his work to fruition.

A second implication is the commission God gives Paul for a special assignment, but also in another sense to all proclaimers of the gospel. It is our task to see that the gospel becomes public information, and not a secret, hidden mystery (1:25). Before Christ men did not know God dreamed of reconciling the universe to himself. It was a hidden plan. But once executed, the plan went public. For the dream to be realized it must be shared with as many humans as possible. Talk about a motivation for evangelism! There it is! "The mystery that has been kept hidden for ages and generations, but is now disclosed to the saints. To them God has chosen to make known among the Gentiles the glorious riches of this mystery, which is Christ in you, the hope of glory" (1:26-27). For Paul a major implication of the Lordship of Christ is proclamation. That is the channel through which Jesus' Lordship over the realm of man will be realized. "We proclaim him" (1:28). This gives the knowledge, the wisdom (as against the wisdom of the incipient Gnostics) to work toward maturity in Christ. Even today some think that to be fed, to attain new spiritual heights, prophecies are needed about unusual, hidden workings of God. One must put in special requests for these spirit filled, maturing insights. They aren't for public possession or consumption. In the thinking of Paul what is needed rather is public proclamation and application of the central salvific facts about the cosmic accomplishments of the cross. Of course sometimes proclamation in the church is so truncated and short-sighted that believers aren't being fed. But what is needed is not an esoteric and flashy messenger. The church desperately needs a deeper plunge into the full implications of the true gospel. The Lordship of Christ obviously calls for a proclamation of the unbelievably good news in the church and in the world.

A third implication for the Lordship of Christ is that those who have received him are "encouraged and united in love" (2:2). Paul worked untiringly that such an end might be attained. For Paul the knowledge of the full mystery of Christ was not special visions, mountain peak experiences, revelations. The full knowledge is apprehended in the manner in which unity and love contribute to God's reconciliation of the world to himself through the Son and the church. Notice 2:2 that the full riches and complete understanding are all tied up in the Christ story. The myth spinners argued otherwise, but Paul countered that it is all right there in the Christ story. Paul believes the story stands out in such bold relief that they won't be led astray. One of the most effective deterents to departures from the gospel is a profound and in-depth explanation of the accomplishments of God in Christ. At least, so Paul thought! Despite the drifting, Paul was not about to count the cause as lost. He believed in the power of a correct presentation of the gospel to turn around an eroding faith. He expresses the confidence he will hear how firm their faith is (2:5). He therefore urgently enjoins the believers to continue in Christ as they received him, rather than according to the spurious versions gaining ground in the region.

The Fullness of the Deity

A fourth implication of the Lordship of Christ is to recognize him alone as Lord, and not get derailed. Paul issued a clarion call to avoid "hollow and deceptive philosophy." The sort of philosophy in mind here involves the *stoicheion.* This Greek word meant many different things. A frequent use of it was the elements. In these days chemists tell us there are 111 or so elements. A common view in Greek antiquity was that the elements are four: earth, water, air, and fire, moving from the heaviest to the lightest. From this basic meaning one jumps to the planets as elements of a different sort. In much of antiquity the planets were assumed to be deities. That is the reason astrology was considered a viable pursuit. If the planets are deities then their movement can indeed be determinative of earthly events. Whether tied with astrology or not, the term *stoicheion* came to be applied to heavenly beings on the order of angels or higher.

The philosophy, therefore of which Paul speaks envisions heavenly beings who are involved in a cosmic drama of salvation. Paul is clear that only one being is involved, Jesus Christ Son of God, and salvation results from the mighty work of God on earth in his death. As such Paul's exclamation is not a condemnation of western philosophy. With few exceptions philosophers have not dabbled in religious myths and cosmic dramas. They categorize these as religion, not philosophy. Various philosophies are antithetical to the gospel, especially twentieth century philosophies. Paul's comment, however, cannot be taken as a blanket condemnation of philosophy and philosophers. Certain philosophers have embraced the gospel and have contributed to its defense.

Philosophy poses a challenge in our time, but perhaps on a popular level, astrology is more of a threat. In the twentieth century not many believe the planets or stars are deities, but various persons do take seriously what they call the insight into human relations provided by horoscopy. These are thought more significant than predictions based on star configurations. Ragardless of which side of astrology is embraced, such deference erodes the Lordship of Christ. He is the supreme cosmic force determining the course of human life. To get bogged down with these lesser powers, whatever their value, is ridiculous when one can get the word straight from the one who rules the universe. To employ an old expression, if one can get it straight from the horse's mouth, why bother with all the clap trap. That was obviously Paul's opinion. "For in Christ all the fullness of the Deity lives in bodily form, and you have been given fullness in Christ, who is head over every power and authority." All these other forces whatever their story and insight cannot compare with Christ. God fully dwells in him.

Nailing It to the Cross

A fifth way of recognizing the Lordship of Christ is as on the mountain of transfiguration to cease homage to Moses and Elijah and serve Jesus only (Mk. 9:8). The problem makers at Colossae apparently were not orthodox Jews. Some, however, came from Jewish ancestry and relished certain Jewish practices such as circumcision (2:11), food regulation (2:16), feast days, and sabbaths (2:16). In Paul's thinking, through his death Christ cancelled these rituals. Clearly the above practices are Jewish, but the "written code" may not be a reference to the law of Moses. In almost every case when Paul refers to the law of Moses he writes *nomos,* preceded by the adjective. What is at stake here therefore may be a code of requirements including items from the Jewish law, but also other regulations not found in the law as mentioned in 2:20-23. This would fit well the thesis we have been pursuing that the objectionable views derived from syncretistic Jews converted to Christianity in the Lycus valley.

What is Paul's message to people who prize such a conglomeration of regulations? He reacts first to circumcision. If the troublers want circumcision, Christians have been circumcised by Christ, but not with the hands. Rather Christ's circumcision is of the heart (See also Romans 2:29). Such circumcision occured when Christians put off their sinful nature (2:11) in baptism (2:12). They were buried with him in baptism and raised through their faith in the power of God who raised him from the dead. This reminds one of Romans 10:9—"If you confess with your mouth, 'Jesus is Lord,' and believe in your heart that God raised him from the dead, you will be saved." Christians were once uncircumcised, but now through Christ's circumcision, they have been made alive, and their sins forgiven. Christ did away with physical circumsicion as well as the regulations offered in the name of other cosmic beings, whether powers or authorities (2:15). He achieved this unprecedented negation by "nailing it to the cross" (2:14). The result was that the other powers with their regulations were disarmed and forced publicly to march in the victory procession behind Christ the victor, thereby recognizing his triumph. The victory was affirmed by the cross. Here as in other cases Paul no doubt has in mind the resurrection which goes hand in hand with the cross.

Since You Died with Christ

The Lordship of Christ last of all rejects any set of regulations not coming from him. If one follows Christ, he does not need to observe Jewish festivals in order to secure his salvation. If he follows Christ he does not need to pay deference to angels. They must in fact pay homage to Christ. If one follows Christ he does not need visions about cosmic dramas and messages (2:18). There is one source for spiritual growth, and that by being subject to the head, namely Christ, "from whom the whole body, supported and held together by its ligaments and sinews, grows as God causes it to grow" (2:19).

Since Christ defused the *stoicheion* (2:20) and commandeered any power they might have, it is puzzling indeed for Christians to be subject to any regulations other than those coming from him. Furthermore, Paul argues, they only appear to aid spiritual growth. In reality, "they lack any value in restraining sensual indulgence" (2:23). We live in a how-to-do-it-age. Trade books abound on every subject, including religion. In Paul's way of thinking Christians would do much better to spend their time with the Christ revealed through the Scriptures. He is the one who has the right answers. Since everything was made through him, including man, he knows the way to get it done so as to come out on top. The Lordship of Christ involves turning away from the bookracks to the Book and finding how-to-do-it from him.

Questions—Chapter 11

1. What is the significance of the church?
2. What does Paul see as the basis for telling our friends and neighbors the good news?
3. What is meant by the *stoicheion* "elemental spirits" RSV?
4. In what sense does Paul oppose philosophy?
5. What is wrong with looking up one's horoscope, from a Christian point of view?
6. What does the cross do to rules, Jewish or other kinds?

Chapter 12

FIXING OUR MOTIVES TO HIS (Colossians 3:1 - 4:6)

Later Gnostics argued that the resurrection occured for the believer when he transferred to the kingdom of light from the kingdom of darkness. For that reason Paul highlights the consequence of the resurrection in Colossians more than in any of his other letters. He mentioned that the result of baptism is that the believer is raised even now with Christ (2:12) and is "alive with Christ" by the power of God (2:13). At the beginning of chapter 3 when Paul turns to the moral and ethical ramifications of the Lordship of Christ, he commences with the observation that believers are "raised with Christ" (3:1). This does not imply, however, that the believer has already arrived, that is, that the future is already here, or as we argued in chapter 8 that in Colossians Paul's eschatology is realized, not inaugurated (see Colossians 1:5; 3:4). He clearly affirms a new reality beyond the end time. "When Christ, who is your life, appears, then you also will appear with him in glory" (3:4).

Set Your Hearts on Things Above

Whereas in Ephesians Paul spelled out the implications of the Christ event in terms of the crucifixion, here he works from the resurrection. The resurrection means the believer is raised with Christ. Just as in Ephesians, "Christ is seated at the right hand of God" (3:1). Whether here too the believer is thought to be seated with Christ is not clear. We could take that to be the implication, but it is not explicit. Now that the believer is raised with Christ, he needs to set his heart on the things that belong to Christ. The call to the Christian is not simply to get his act right. Both Jesus and Paul emphasize that if one has his heart with God, if that is where he really lives, if that is what really excites him, then his act will straighten itself out. The mind likewise is to be set on things above (3:2). One is to get his thoughts in the Christian framework. Right thoughts are certainly imperative for right commitment. The translation "heart" (3:1) and "mind" (3:2) (NIV) may be misleading inasmuch as "heart" is not in the Greek text. Paul does not say first get your heart attuned to God, then your mind. The point in 3:1 is a repeat, but Paul adds "not on earthly things." The question is, what specifically is the difference? Is centering on heavenly things sitting around contemplating what heaven is like, whether the throne is made of walnut, the tree of life a cottonwood, and streets solid or simply gold plate, who wrote the songs of praise, and what are the names of other angels in addition to Gabriel and Michael? As it turns out, setting our minds on things above is not to contemplate the contours of heaven. Rather, it is to think about God's ways of relating to people here.

Paul does, however, refer to a death of the believer. Because in Christ he died, his pre-Christian attitudes and actions have disappeared. The past for many hangs as an albatross around their neck. Sometimes they say, "Oh, if I could only live down my past." Paul says, not only can you live down your past, you can make it disappear completely. You can do so by accepting the forgiveness made available by the death of Christ. When a person becomes a Christian, others may still think of him in terms of his past. But God thinks differently. The past is gone. The light now shining on their life is reflected from the son of God. "Your life is now hidden with Christ in God." This means that the old life with its ways, its thoughts, has disappeared. Now even friends, if they are willing to look, see not the old person, but the new, the one radiating ways of Christ. The end result is that as Christ's, one's life subjugated to his, the believer will also appear with him in glory (3:4). Christ is coming again for those who are his. Because they are hidden in him, he will return to the Father and present those who are his.

Put to Death

Since in Christ one was cut adrift from his past, he must let it disappear over the horizon. He must erase it from his life—put it to death (3:5). From Paul's statement it is clear that being forgiven of sin does not stop it. Being in Christ does not automatically and immediately make one a saint in thought and action. A lot of effort is involved in saint making. It requires action on God's part and on our part. We don't have to worry about God. He will come through. If we have problems with sin, it isn't God's fault, as if he is unable or unwilling. The problem is ours. If we really turn over our life, everything we have and are, to God, open the door and let him help us get rid of sin, he will. The initiative is ours. God is waiting, willing, and able. Regardless of what people say, you can help it, or better, you can let God help it. Regardless of what people say, the devil didn't make you do it. Rather, you let the devil make you do it. The means are available for us to live the way God wants us to live. "Put to death, therefore, whatever belongs to your earthly nature" (3:5).

Paul now lists a series of actions and attitudes which belong to an earthly nature. In Ephesians these were actions destroying unity. In Colossians where the stress is not so much on unity as on the right perception of Christ and the right life following there from, the effort is to distinguish what is earthly from what is heavenly. What common denominator if any do we find in the list of earthly attributes? One attitude seems to stand out: "I see it, I want it." This outlook presupposes that life is fulfilled by struggling for and taking what I really want in the world about. In this manner the things of this world become ends in themselves. The world and its contents become objects of worship. As Paul puts it in Romans, the one motivated by his earthly nature worships and serves "created things rather than the Creator—who is forever praised" (Rom. 1:25).

Of those items comprising the earthly nature, Paul lists two groups of five. The things above consist of one grouping of five (3:12). The number is not significant in itself. It makes clear that Paul does not propose to put out an exhaustive catalogue in either case. He offers rather examples of the differences so the reader can get the drift and expand into other specifics on his own.

To engage in sexual immorality is to think sex is an end in itself (3:5). Sex, which is created by God, is to be used for his purposes which are to replenish the earth and to manifest holy love. Immorality is taking what one wants. It is to make a god out of something in the world. Impurity is to engage in an activity foreign to the known ways of God, but in this case is tied with sexual impurity. Persons who are sex-driven spend most of their waking hours dreaming about and pursuing sexual relationships. They have little time left to think about God and his work in the world. Lust and evil desires likewise have to do with sexual improprieties. One of the false deities (stoicheion?) is that of sex as an overpowering passion. The Greeks even had a name for the god, *Eros.* The Christian is subject to no god, except the Lord God. The last item, that is, greed, is not in the same category as the four previous, yet sexual desire is sometimes characterized by greed, that is, to make a conquest of as many persons as possible. Greed involves cornering the market on what one is most interested in in this world. It is as if the things of this world have meaning in themselves, whether it be land, silver, commodities, horses, power, or antiques! Such greed is idolatry. It is to worship the creation rather than the Creator. Such worship detracts from the worship of the true God. "You cannot worship God and mammon" (Matt. 6:24). God is a jealous God. He cannot and will not permit men to make a God out of mammon. For this reason his wrath is coming (3:6).

In the second series Paul identifies traits in which people are treated as things. To do so is to say that one's own desires take precedence. People hence become objects or means to one's own ends. "You must rid yourselves of all such things as these: anger, rage, malice, slander, and filthy language from your lips" (3:8). Lying falls into the same category (3:9). All ten characteristics are informed by the ways of the earth, not the ways of God. The new self "is renewed in knowledge in the image of its Creator" (3:10). In the kingdom of God each person regardless of background has worth in themselves because of God. They are to be treated as brothers because of Christ. Paul listed the various ethnic factions in his world (3:11). Ours are different, but we too must overcome treating people as things because they are not our kind. All those in Christ Jesus are our kind.

The Things Above

God's people need to remember who they are. They are

"God's chosen people, holy and dearly loved" (3:12). It now emerges in the five traits that to set one's mind on things above is not to think about the geography, fixtures, or creatures in heaven. It is rather to think on the characteristics of God and how they can be replicated in one's relationships with others. Not only did the unprecedented act of God take place on earth, the human response to God takes place on earth. To set one's heart on the things above does not take us out of this world. It takes us rather away from an earthly nature, to treat people and things as God would treat them. The five traits to be put on are the traits of God. First is compassion. Jesus was above all a person of compassion for lepers, outcasts, blind and otherwise incapacitated persons, both Jew and Gentile. Jesus was also kind. He was kind to little children and people on the road who stopped him. Surely, Jesus likewise was humble, gentle, and patient. To be thinking heavenly thoughts is to think about how one can bring love, patience and so on, to inform one's relations with others in the world. One will use the things of this world. That is why God made them. He will, however, love the people in the world. He will be God's ambassador to people. He will treat them as God treats them.

Paul (3:12) continues with what it is like to be raised with Christ. It is to put up with and bear the foibles and needs of others. It is to forgive as the Lord already has forgiven. Love, he says, is the umbrella virtue which binds all the others together. We are reminded of, "And now these three remain: faith, hope and love. But the greatest of these is love" (1 Cor. 13:13). The one who thinks on heavenly things will let the peace of Christ rule in his heart. He will be a thankful person. The person who realizes all that God has done for him will be continually filled with gratitude and thanksgiving. He will be a person who regularly contemplates the word of Christ and shares it with others in word and song. The one who sets his mind on things above always reflects on what he is about to do or say, or has done or said, to see if it is done in the name of the Lord Jesus (Col. 3:17). One is constantly grateful for what he has done and impressed that he has been invited to follow suit. He therefore is in frequent thanks to the Father through him (3:17).

To set one's mind on things above is in addition to be

Jesus-like in marriage, family, and occupation. Because we covered these matters at length in Ephesians, we will not go into details here. In Colossians Paul sets out essentially the same instructions. Here likewise he premises these relationships on submission. "Wives, submit to your husbands, as is fitting in the Lord" (3:18). In Colossians, however, the groundwork isn't laid for that submission as in Ephesians. Paul hasn't spelled out the giving, submitting, sacrificing, and love of Christ for his people and the church as in Ephesians. We remind ourselves that in Colossians Paul is spelling out the implications of being raised with Christ. To be raised with him is to act like him and that is enough in Colossians.

Devote Yourselves to Prayer

Paul closes the application section with a charge to the believers to be God's praying people. In prayer in a unique sense one sets his mind on things above. When we pray we think about God's ways, what he wants to hear, and what he wants us to be. Prayer is premised on watching, that is, being sensitive to how God is working things out, and thankfulness. Though Paul's work has been extremely successful, he is extremely sensitive to the fact that it was God who accomplished it through him. He therefore requests prayers in behalf of his Roman imprisonment ministry. Last, he requests that they use Christ-like judgment, that is, be wise, in their relationships with outsiders to create the best situation from which to speak of the Lord (4:5). The conversation of the Christian should reflect the grace of God. It should also not be dull and bland, but seasoned with salt; that is, interesting, vigorous, and with carefully chosen words. In that manner God's work will be disclosed and a satisfactory answer supplied (4:6).

Questions—Chapter 12

1. What are the implications of the resurrection in Colossians?

2. What does it mean to "set our mind on things above"?

3. How do we overcome sin?

4. What is basic to sin in Colossians 3?

5. Why is prayer so important in Paul's thinking?

Chapter 13

WORKING WITH PAUL (Colossians 4:7-15)

The end of Colossians mentions ten persons who in some way or another were involved with Paul in ministry. Paul obviously was an effective evangelizer and church planter. He was impressive in working with people. He possibly was even more successful in getting those he converted to convert others. The end of Colossians makes it obvious that he was no lone wolf. He did not need the encouragement of a large body of Christians so as to function. But he did need a support group. He built his own, as is clear from the end of Colossians.

What if we set out to be a worker in the kingdom like Paul, "the kingdom of the Son he loves" (1:13)? Paul would like that. In fact he would do everything in his power to help us get started and encourage us. He believed, by the way, that our call is to do our best in God's great work of reconciliation. The saints—that's us—have our work cut out. Once we know "the mystery that has been kept hidden for ages and generations," it is our task to pass the word along. "To them," that is, the saints, namely us, "God has chosen to make known among the Gentiles the glorious riches of this mystery, which is Christ in you, the hope of glory" (1:27).

What would it be like to learn discipleship from Paul? We would learn it no doubt by working with Paul, at least numerous people did. What if we set out to learn from Paul, to apprentice under him? From reading Paul's letters it is apparent we would notice something immediately. Paul cared. We have previously mentioned that Paul was the true believer. He was also a true carer. He cared because he was convinced beyond a doubt that God cared. That was what the gospel is about, that God cared so much he sent his only Son. Paul believed God cared for him. He likewise believed that he cared for every man and woman. Paul cared because God cared. Paul for that reason taught others to care. That is what discipleship is about. Discipleship is caring. Working with Paul therefore is receiving and giving care.

What do we learn specifically from going with Paul? That is what the rest of this chapter is about. A fitting conclusion to Ephesians and Colossians is focused on discipleship and discipling. Paul expected such a result from his letters. "Wake up, O sleeper, rise from the dead, and Christ will shine on you" (Eph. 5:14). In the rest of this chapter we are going to depart somewhat from the procedure thus far. Rather than trying to follow the text of Colossians 4:7-15, we are going to make eleven observations on what it would be like to work with Paul. We have much to learn from this great and deeply committed man. This is so whatever our role. Not every observation applies to each disciple, but some do, and in certain cases all.

1. *Paul cared so much he shared the Christ mystery with all comers.* To the Roman Christians he wrote, "I am obligated both to Greeks and non-Greeks, both to the wise and the foolish. That is why I am so eager to preach the gospel also to you who are at Rome" (Rom. 1:14,15). He was obligated because of what God had done for him. "But by the grace of God I am what I am, and his grace to me was not without effect" (1 Cor. 15:10). He was also obligated because he was given a special trust to share God's good news. "So then, men ought to regard us as servants of Christ and as those entrusted with the secret things of God. Now it is required that those who have been given a trust must prove faithful" (1 Cor. 4:2). "Surely you have heard about the administration of God's grace that was given to me for you." So great upon Paul was the weight of God's work and his care that he rejoiced in suffering for the gospel. "Now I rejoice in what was suffered for you, and I fill up in my flesh what is still lacking in regard to Christ's afflictions, for the sake of his body, which is the church. I have become its servant by the commission God gave me to present to you the work of God in its fullness" (Col. 1:24,25). Paul cared for people as he expresses for the Jews. "I have great sorrow and unceasing anguish in my heart. For I

could wish that I myself were cursed and cut off from Christ for the sake of my brothers, those of my own race, the people of Israel" (Rom. 9:2-4). As the result of his care he won numerous people to the Lord, "from Jerusalem to Illyricum" (Rom. 15:19). These he gathered into caring bodies. "Be devoted to one another in brotherly love. Honor one another above yourselves" (Rom. 12:10).

2. *He picked out people for special training.* We know of several persons handpicked by Paul for servanthood in caring ministry. One was Epaphras, "our dear fellow servant, who is a faithful minister of Christ on our behalf" (Col. 1:7). We know several names: Timothy, Titus, Silvanus, Tychicus, Aristarchus, Mark. Of surprise to some is that women were included. "I plead with Euodia and I plead with Syntyche to agree with each other in the Lord. Yes, and I ask you, loyal yokefellow, help these women who have contended at my side in the cause of the gospel, along with Clement and the rest of my fellow workers" (Phil. 4:2,3). All these persons Paul trained in a caring ministry. Paul no doubt spent time with those who hurt, but not just with them. He spent an inordinate amount of time training others. It is said that some executives fail because they spend most of their time trying to make ineffective persons more effective. Paul did not ignore persons with problems, but he shared much of his time and energies with committed people who in turn could teach others to care.

3. *Paul gave these people experience in multiple situations.* In order to spread the caring gospel Paul invited leaders in training to travel with him personally. One of the first was Mark the cousin of Barnabas. These two came to a parting of the ways, but by the time Colossians was written Mark was with Paul and doing an effective work. One of Paul's most constant and trusted companions was Timothy. Not only did on the job training call attention to Paul as a model, it also provided a support group which could take on multiple tasks and supply mutual encouragement. Paul believed that the most effective way of teaching is to involve others in our work so they can see how we do it. Paul did not teach in an isolated classroom. He taught in the classroom of life.

4. *Paul sent converts back to teach their own people.* A prime example is Epaphras who brought God's announcement

to those in the Lycus Valley (Col. 1:7, 4:12). Paul not only planted churches he trained his converts to plant churches. In that way his efforts were multiplied many times over. In order to prepare these persons for the task Paul utilized prime people time. He was not adverse to writing and asking people to read when it served a purpose, but he mostly trained his co-workers through personal contact. They did not need a Pauline manual. They had a Pauline model.

5. *Paul revisited churches and implemented communication channels.* Paul made a lifetime commitment to those he brought to Jesus Christ. He revisited churches as often as circumstances permitted. To the church in Corinth he wrote, "After I go through Macedonia, I will come to you—for I will be going through Macedonia. Perhaps I will stay with you awhile, or even spend the winter, so that you can help me on my journey, wherever I go" (1 Cor. 16:5,6). Sometimes we hesitate to visit people we have once shared the gospel with under the view that perhaps they will not be that anxious to see us. Some did not relish Paul's visits but he returned anyway, because he cared. Through his visits Paul kept up with the churches. He taught the same concern to his associates. Furthermore he encouraged the churches to keep in communication with each other. He asked the churches in the Lycus Valley to exchange the letters he wrote (Col. 4:16).

6. *Paul arranged church visits for his co-workers.* Paul established caring networks among his workers. He had them visit the various churches to express his and their concern and work on any problems. To the church at Philippi he wrote, "I hope in the Lord Jesus to send Timothy to you soon, that I also may be cheered when I receive news about you. I have no one else like him, who takes a genuine interest in your welfare. . . . But I think it is necessary to send back to you Epaphroditus, my brother, fellow worker and fellow soldier, who is also your messenger, whom you sent to take care of my needs. For he longs for all of you and is distressed because you heard he was ill" (Phil. 3:19-26). This indeed shows that Paul was quite successful in instilling his own concern in his apprentices. It also shows that Paul had established communication channels. The Philippians heard that their brother Epaphroditus was ill, even over that long distance.

7. *Paul kept up with the churches through personal oral messages.* Tychicus was not to just deliver a letter to the Colossians. He was to explain in detail Paul's situation. "I am sending him to you for the express purpose that you may know about our circumstances and that he may encourage your hearts." Paul likewise planned to send Timothy and Apollos to Corinth. "If Timothy comes, see to it that he has nothing to fear while he is with you, for he is carrying on the work of the Lord, just as I am. . . . Send him on his way in peace so that he may return to me. I am expecting him along with the brothers. Now about our brother Apollos: I strongly urged him to go to you with the brothers. He was quite unwilling to go now, but he will go when he has the opportunity" (1 Cor. 16:10-12).

8. *Paul wrote letters to the churches.* If one knows anything about Paul, he knows that he wrote letters. In fact, by reading through his letters we know he wrote far more than have been preserved. Paul showed his concern for the persons he brought to Christ by writing letters to encourage them, to straighten out misunderstandings, and to instruct them in the faith. None of Paul's churches could claim he neglected them. Before long either one of his fellow workers would show up, a letter, or both. He even sent letters to churches started by his converts such as the letter to the Colossians. When Paul wrote he included greetings by his fellow workers. We have a series of these at the end of Colossians (Col. 4:10-12).

9. *To show his support and concern for his converts, Paul communicated with their converts.* A prime example once again is the church in the Lycus Valley. These churches were planted by Paul's converts. But he took a personal interest in them. Not only did he correspond, but he planned a visit at a later date. To Philemon, Onesimus' master, he wrote, "And one thing more: Prepare a guest room for me, because I hope to be restored to you in answer to your prayers" (Philemon 22).

10. *Paul was effective in group evangelism.* Some persons do effective work by themselves, but are unable to share and join in with co-workers. Paul was committed to getting along with people. He thought the gospel called people to share and love. Therefore he very seldomly launched a work by himself. We have already quoted the Philippians passage in which women were involved (Phil. 4:2,3). Paul delighted in sharing

the work, and the honors.

11. *The concern of Paul for his and their converts was continually expressed in prayer.* Not only did Paul communicate with the believers, he communicated with God about them. To the Philippians he wrote, "I thank my God every time I remember you. In all my prayers for all of you, I always pray with joy because of your partnership in the gospel from the first day until now" (Phil. 1:3-5). Paul had himself planted the church in Philippi. He had not been to Colossae, nevertheless he prayed for them. "For this reason, since the day we heard about you, we have not stopped praying for you and asking God to fill you with the knowledge of his will through all spiritual wisdom and understanding" (Col. 1:9). Not only did he pray, he encouraged his apprentices and fellow workers to do the same. About Epaphras Paul wrote the Colossians, "He is always wrestling in prayer for you, that you may stand firm in all the will of God, mature and fully assured" (Col. 4:12).

Many other observations could be made, but these indeed show Paul as a deeply caring person for those who were won to the good news of God's work in Jesus Christ. These observations I believe have far-reaching implications for preachers, elders, missionaries, and churches. You say, "That's nice. But I'm not a preacher, so they aren't very helpful to me." But that's where you're wrong. Each Christian has his or her ministry—a caring ministry. You have been so blessed by God you can't help but share his goodness with others. And once you reach people for the Lord, Paul says keep up with them in every way possible. If they move, write, visit, call. When they bring people to the Lord, get acquainted with them even if they live at a distance. Call, write, visit. Get involved with others in sharing the gospel, perhaps in a home Bible study or in whatever way possible.

It is appropriate to end this book with Paul's prayer for the believers in Colossae: "And we pray this in order that you may live a life worthy of the Lord and may please him in every way: bearing fruit in every good work, growing in the knowledge of God, being strengthened with all power according to his glorious might so that you may have great endurance and patience, and joyfully giving thanks to the Father, who has qualified you to share in the inheritance of the saints in the kingdom of light" (Col. 1:10-12).

Questions—Chapter 13

1. Does Paul invite people—us included—to be co-workers with him?
2. How did Paul plant churches?
3. How did Paul nourish churches?
4. How did Paul train future preachers?
5. What characteristic did he attempt to implant?
6. Can we apply any or all of Paul's approaches?